P9-CKY-065

DEC 19 2002

JUN 2 8 2024

PROPERTY OF:
DAVID O. McKAY LIBRARY
BYU-IDAHO
REXBURG ID 83460-0405

THE LITTLE THEATRE ON THE SQUARE

THE
LITTLE THEATRE
ON THE SQUARE

Four Decades of a Small-Town
Equity Theatre

Beth Conway Shervey
With a Foreword by Peter Palmer

SOUTHERN ILLINOIS UNIVERSITY PRESS
CARBONDALE AND EDWARDSVILLE

Copyright © 2000 by the Board of Trustees,
Southern Illinois University
All rights reserved
Printed in the United States of America
03 02 01 00   4 3 2 1

Library of Congress Cataloging-in-Publication Data
Shervey, Beth Conway, 1964–
    The Little Theatre on the Square : four decades of a small-town Equity theatre /
Beth Conway Shervey ; with a foreword by Peter Palmer.
        p. cm.
    Includes bibliographical references and index.
    1. Little Theatre on the Square (Sullivan, Ill.) 2. Theater—Illinois—Sullivan—
History—20th century. I. Title.

PN2277.S832 L58 2000
792'.09773'675—dc21
                                                            00-036543
    ISBN 0-8093-2354-0 (alk. paper)
    ISBN 0-8093-2355-9 (pbk. : alk. paper)

The paper used in this publication meets the minimum requirements of American
National Standard for Information Sciences—Permanence of Paper for Printed Library
Materials, ANSI Z39.48-1992. ♾

TO MY PARENTS WITH LOVE

CONTENTS

———❦———

ILLUSTRATIONS

Following page 26

The Grand Theatre in 1962.

The Moultrie County Courthouse in the early 1960s.

Mark Rydell, star of *The Glass Menagerie,* in 1962.

Peter Palmer first appeared at The Little Theatre in 1962.

Ann B. Davis in *Everybody Loves Opal* in 1963.

Margaret Truman with Ron Rogers in *Late Love* in 1963.

Inis Little, mother of Guy S. Little Jr., with Joe E. Brown in
    Harvey in 1963.

Linda Darnell appearing in *Janus* in 1964.

John Carradine starred in *Dracula* in 1965 and in *Oliver* in 1966.

Rosemary Prinz in *Mary, Mary* in 1965.

Guy S. Little Jr. with his daughter, Vanessa, and son, Sean, in a
    production of *Carousel* in 1966.

Jerili Little with Dennis Weaver in *Catch Me If You Can* in 1966.

Peter Palmer with Sen. Charles Percy and Aniko Farrell in 1966.

Guy S. Little Jr. in 1967.

Mercedes McCambridge in *Who's Afraid of Virginia Woolf?* in
    1967.

Rosemary Prinz signs autographs in 1967.

Pat and Eloise O'Brien from a publicity still for *Holiday for Lovers* in 1969.

Following page 76

Bob Crane with apprentices in 1971.

Apprentices in front of the rehearsal hall in 1971.

Set designer Bob Soule in 1971.

Margaret Hamilton and Ann Miller in *Blithe Spirit* in 1973.

Ann Miller in 1973.

Harve Presnell in *On a Clear Day You Can See Forever* in 1973.

Bill Hayes with costar in *The Fantasticks* in 1973.

Lesley Ann Warren in *Irma La Douce* in 1973.

Feature photograph from the *Moultrie County News* promoting the production of *Hair* in 1974.

The main players from *Hair* in 1974.

The Tribe from *Hair* in 1974.

Leonard Nimoy in *One Flew over the Cuckoo's Nest* in 1974.

Isabel Sanford and Lillian Lehman in *And Mama Makes Three* in 1977.

Stubby Kaye in *Fiddler on the Roof* in 1977.

Charles Bell and Shannon McHugh in *Seven Brides for Seven Brothers* in 1988.

Glen Washington with the cast of *Joseph and the Amazing Technicolor Dreamcoat* in 1988.

Artistic director M. Seth Reines with Jeff Talbott and Jack Milo in 1988.

Executive director Leonard Anderson in *Carousel* in 1994.

The cast of *West Side Story* in 1992.

Jack Milo and Michael Haws in *A Funny Thing Happened on the Way to the Forum* in 1996.

FOREWORD

In so many ways, I feel that Sullivan, Illinois, is my hometown. Well, Sullivan isn't really, because I was born in Milwaukee and raised mostly in St. Louis, and I spent four years at the University of Illinois. However, when I look back on my professional life and an almost fifty-year (and sometimes illustrious) career, I surely can claim I grew up in Sullivan.

I first became familiar with Sullivan in the spring of 1953 when I arrived at the Sullivan Country Club as part of a Fighting Illini football promotional jaunt to raise money for scholarships and to sell tickets for the football season. Ray Eliot, our head coach, and Burt Ingwerson, my line coach, would make a pep talk and introduce me as the "first music major to letter in football." I would then get up and sing "The Wiffenpoof Song" with Ray, followed by my doing a couple of solos. At that time, I met the "movers and shakers" of Sullivan, and many of them would later become my closest friends.

The Little Theatre, of course, was founded by Guy and Jerri Little. I had known Jerri at the University of Illinois, and I had done my first book show, *Roberta,* with her in 1952. I had also met Guy and Jerri by chance in the late 1950s on a subway train in New York. It was shortly after they had been married, and they had told me that they were about to open The Little Theatre in Sullivan.

The Little Theatre was not under a union contract and could hire professional actors only under extreme limitations. Since I had already done *Li'l Abner* on Broadway and in the movie, I could not work there. However, I had heard very good reports through my voice teacher, U. of I. professor Bruce Foote, when he played Emile de Becque in *South Pacific*. He had written to me that they were doing first-class productions and that I should work there when I got the chance. I got the chance when The Little Theatre joined Equity and Guy asked me to do *Oklahoma!* in 1962.

One has to remember that I had done some pretty heady stuff since the first time I had been to Sullivan, like opening a couple of home games at the U. of I. with the national anthem in full football uniform and being a member of the 1953 Big Ten championship team. I had also won a talent contest over WGN radio and received a trip to Hollywood. I got offers from Universal and MGM to enter their talent training programs. At the same time, I received another offer for a two-year, noncancelable contract with the U.S. Army. There, I won the All-Army Entertainment Contest and appeared on *The Ed Sullivan Show*. Being seen on that show, I was asked to create the role of Li'l Abner in the Broadway production, and the national tour took me on an extended run in Las Vegas. I then recreated the role in the Paramount movie, and that exposure led to several more guest appearances on the top variety shows and sitcoms of the day. I also took my nightclub act to such posh places as the Drake in Chicago, the Shamrock Hilton in Houston, and the Waldorf-Astoria in New York City.

By 1962, I am sure I was pretty full of myself. But I will tell you, that headiness ended when I came "home" to Sullivan. My first day went something like this. I arrived at the Champaign airport, and Guy and Jerri Little drove the sixty miles to Sullivan. They showed me The Little Theatre and then on to Art and Mamie Palmer's home, where the theatre put up the "stars." The Palmers were not related to me, but they would become close friends and my surrogate aunt and uncle. From there it was on to Jibby's for dinner. Jibby's was then owned by Jibby and Ruth Florini, and it was the only late-night spot in Sullivan. Through the years, they and their family would become more like "kissin' cousins."

Bo Woods, a local insurance guy, came in to say hello, and he reminded me that I had met him my first time around in 1953. He invited me to a stag party in my honor at the Sullivan Country

Club pool that night. Art Palmer drove me out, and there was not one light to be seen. I could see the shadows of the men around the pool. As we swung into a parking place, the headlights made a sweep of the pool, and I could see all those shadows were in the buff. "Have a beer, take off your clothes, and have a swim" was the order of the night. I have to tell you, one gets to know others very well and rather quickly when one discusses this and that in the nude. That was my first day in Sullivan.

My first show there was *Oklahoma!,* and I had the idea of coming in from the rear of the house down the right aisle singing "Oh, What a Beautiful Mornin'." And I can remember the audience reaching out to shake my hand. Many wonderful musicals followed, a couple of which I didn't think I was quite right for. However, Guy said, "Peter, you are right for the part, and it is time for you to do parts you are capable of doing."

I remember getting engaged to actress-singer and former Miss Canada Aniko Farrell and announcing my wedding plans in front of The Little Theatre. Guy let Aniko do her first leading role as my leading lady in *Brigadoon,* and many musicals starring the Palmers followed. I can remember a farm couple who had waited for us at the stage door, and when they saw us, they burst into tears. Aniko and I ushered them into our dressing room, and they showed us a torn piece of paper with our autographs on it. We realized that we had signed it for a young soldier when we had made a USO tour of Vietnam the previous year. "Mom" told us that he had been killed, and when the Army sent his stuff back, the autographs were on top of his most personal possessions. They had come to see us and tell us. There were a lot of tears that night.

Guy and Jerri would work all year, using their extensive talents singing, acting out, showing movies and slides, anything to promote The Little Theatre On The Square to anyone who would sit and listen. They would send the stars and Sullivan's "favorites" all over central Illinois to promote their performances and the upcoming shows. I got the idea, after each show and while still in costume, of jumping on the buses and thanking the audience members for coming and supporting the theatre. Each year there were more buses. Guy and Jerri were inspirational.

Mostly I remember no one was ever treated like a "star." If you wanted to be left alone, the townsfolk left you alone. If you wanted to be friendly, they were more than willing to accept it and take you in and be friends. The home folks would always let me know if I had gained or lost weight, if my hair was too long or too short, and if they liked the show or not, and they always stated it with love. I always felt like I had come back home.

The Little Theatre On The Square was very special to me as it was to so many apprentices, actors, and directors who have worked there. For me, Sullivan was like the musical play about the mystical town of Brigadoon, which appeared once every hundred years. However, it really appeared to me, and later to my wife Aniko, once a year in the summer when I came back to do a musical for Guy. Not only did Aniko and I learn much about our craft at The Little Theatre, we also got to see our friends in Sullivan, as well as those from St. Louis, the U. of I., and the whole surrounding area. My wife and I still go back to Sullivan to see them all and to polish our "stars" in front of the theatre. They are still doing wonderful, quality shows in my "hometown" at The Little Theatre On The Square. It only makes me wish I had it all to do over again. It's about time someone wrote a book about The Little Theatre On The Square.

PETER PALMER

PREFACE

When I was a child growing up in Sullivan, The Little Theatre On The Square was as much of a landmark around Sullivan as the library or the grocery store. During summers, attending productions of The Children's Theatre on any given Saturday was as taken for granted as televised cartoons or afternoons at the swimming pool. As a high school student working at the theatre, first as an usher then as the photographer's assistant, I did not take the existence of the theatre in town as at all unusual. I realized the world inside the theatre was antithetical to most things I had known, but I assumed such contradictions were part of life in most towns. Time and distance from Moultrie County put all of that into a much different perspective.

An Equity theatre in a town of four thousand people is exceptional, and it certainly affected how I perceived life in Sullivan. Over the years the question began to emerge: If my limited involvement with the theatre so shaped my own perceptions, what effect has it had on people who have lived in the area for years or even decades?

It seemed to me, as a writer and oral historian, that the people to best answer the question were those who bridged the gap between "townie" and "showdog," area residents who were also involved with the theatre. Through their stories emerges a history of the theatre put in the context of life in Sullivan. Consequently, the broader consequences—cultural, social, and political—of an Equity theatre in a town like Sullivan are examined.

As one who briefly bridged that gap, I am fortunate to bring to this work a familiarity an outsider would be unlikely to possess and access to information unobtainable by most people. Most of the people I interviewed have known me since I was in grade school. They were friends and colleagues of my parents, former teachers, parents of my classmates, and just people one becomes acquainted with growing up in a small town. What was unexpected was the satisfaction of getting to know, as an adult, many of the people I was surrounded by as a child.

Consequently, any lingering ideas I had had of small-town life as anything other than intrinsically complex and dynamic quickly disappeared. The outcome is, I hope, a clear-sighted look at where the stories of a community and of one of its institutions intersect.

I am deeply indebted to those people who agreed to be interviewed and consented to let their stories be used in this book. The one notable exception, unfortunately, is Guy S. Little Jr., who previously had graciously granted me a lengthy taped interview for my research, for which I am most grateful, but who has refused to let any of the material be used for this book. I was, however, able to use material from the many interviews he has given to newspapers since 1957.

There are many other people whom I must acknowledge. Continued appreciation goes to Leonard Anderson and M. Seth Reines, who currently face the challenge of keeping the ideal of the theatre alive.

Once again, I owe infinite recognition to those Sullivan and area residents who participated in this project: Ron and Sharon White, Margaret Hollowell, Jibby and Ruth Florini, Joe and Jean Florini, Pauline Rowles, Dick Isaacs, Mamie Palmer, Emilee Best, and Bill and Marilyn Stubblefield.

Special thanks go to all the members of the theatre company who provided that crucial view of life in Sullivan from the "show-dog" perspective, especially Jack Milo, Michael Haws, and Chuck Bell, who saw things from both sides.

I owe much to those at Bowling Green State University who

helped to make this book possible: Don McQuarie, Ron Shields, Art Neal, and especially, Bill Grant.

Last, but certainly not least, are those people who have been along for almost the entire voyage and to whom I owe a debt of gratitude I can only hope someday to repay: Marion Best, David Mobley, and my husband, Scott Stirling.

1

THE SIGNIFICANCE OF THEATRE IN THE CORN BELT

O n 3 July 1957, The Little Theatre On The Square* presented *Brigadoon* in Sullivan, Illinois, making a childhood dream of its founder, Guy S. Little Jr., come true. As a boy growing up in Sullivan, Little had dreamed of owning a theatre, preferably someplace in the Midwest. With good fortune, he was able to open his theatre at the age of twenty-one in his hometown, fresh from graduate study and theatre work in New York. From these providential beginnings, the story of the theatre's eventual success and status as the only Equity house between Chicago and St. Louis, located in a town with one stoplight, has taken on mythic proportions. What has not been told is the significance of such a theatre in a community like Sullivan and the collective effect it has had over the years. The effect of the theatre has gone beyond an individual's dreams coming true; it has indelibly changed the cultural landscape of a central Illinois farming town. The Little Theatre provided professional productions but also introduced into Sullivan a theatrical

---

*From 1957 to 1962, the theatre in Sullivan was called Summer of Musicals at the Grand Theatre. Guy S. Little Jr. bought the theatre in 1963 and changed the name to The Little Theatre–On The Square. Over the years, there have been variations in how the full name of the theatre looks. Currently in use is The Little Theatre On The Square. The full name is used interchangeably with the shortened title, The Little Theatre, including references to the first six seasons.

community whose lifestyles and values were quite different from the traditions of a small Midwestern town.

On the surface, Sullivan—then and now—is no different from many other Midwestern farming communities. The central business district surrounds the courthouse square. The courthouse is an early-twentieth-century, three-story structure with a rotunda and clocks facing each side of the square. Except for grain elevators and water towers, it is the tallest structure in the county. The first business on the square to begin its day is the Spot, a diner that opens at 5:00 A.M. to serve biscuits and gravy to farmers and other locals. The Little Theatre, nestled next to the Spot on the north side of the square, could easily pass as a typical community theatre, which, of course, it is not.

Visible evidence of the theatre's history and continuing status as an Equity house is not as apparent as one would expect, being generally limited to a few businesses that feature autographed photographs of stars. A more recent reminder is the "Sidewalk of the Stars," marble plaques with actors' names and the years they appeared cemented into the sidewalk that fronts the square's businesses. One need only to scratch just beneath the surface of Sullivan, however, and forty years of local stories and events, many quite incongruous with small-town life, appear like fragments at an archaeological dig.

For many Sullivan and area residents, The Little Theatre On The Square has simply been taken for granted. These people have not been involved with the theatre other than as audience members, and sometimes not even that. Few have been vocally or violently opposed to the theatre; rather, the common feeling has been one of ambivalence or simply indifference. Others, however, have welcomed the theatre passionately for any number of reasons and at different times in the theatre's existence. Many have become very personally involved. What they got out of their alliances with the theatre ranged from social to artistic to personal to civic satisfaction, and the consequences, for many, have outlived their contact with the theatre and even their lives in town. The theatre, accordingly, has assumed a unique position in each person's memory and takes an individual form with each retelling of a story.

The Little Theatre also put Sullivan on the map. As area people traveled about the country and mentioned where they were from, a typical response was, "Oh, Sullivan . . . you mean that place with that theatre." Especially after the theatre began featuring stars, it drew attention from outlying media, as well as busloads of audience members. It is doubtful that few, if any, would complain about the attention it drew to Sullivan. The *reasons,* however, for which the theatre and, consequently, Sullivan were known occasionally spawned indignation among groups of residents. After all, as Wilbur Zelinsky (1988) notes, the very notion of hometown pride extends beyond the city limits.

BRIGADOON REDEFINED

One need not look far to find the irony in The Little Theatre's choice for its maiden production. Like the mythical Scottish village of Brigadoon, Sullivan, like many other small towns, was insulated against outside forces. In 1957, Sullivan held firmly to the bosom of Eisenhower's America and the buttoned-down values it represented. The local Women's Christian Temperance Union chapter was going strong, and teachers were told to stay out of taverns; athletics was the informal religion, and the variations of Protestantism were the formal ones; Catholics were the minority and *everyone* was the color of Wonder Bread.

The parallel with the musical can be taken one step further: Strangers bring change to both Brigadoon and Sullivan. That, however, is where the similarities end. In *Brigadoon,* the protagonist was reluctantly allowed back in and then the village latched its shutters for another century. Sullivan, on the other hand, with the theatre as welcome mat, actively sought to bring in outsiders and keep them coming.

Over the years, The Little Theatre On The Square has brought many new people to town—performers, techies, audience members, and sightseers. It also has been a cultural oddity that enticed a few people to move to Sullivan and gave more than a few reasons to stay. People in all these capacities influenced the area, but those outsiders who worked for the theatre and the Sullivan residents who became part of the theatre sphere had the strongest and most lasting impact.

Instead of slowing down time, as happened to the villagers of Brigadoon, The Little Theatre, in a sense, has accelerated it. The theatre created a cultural ripple, a time warp through which social forces often at odds with perceived values of small-town life trav-

eled. This is not to say that, were it not for the theatre, residents of
Sullivan would never have faced issues like racism, homophobia,
urban liberalism, and even alcohol consumption. The point is that
the existence of an Equity theatre and, especially, the people associated with it, has accelerated the rate at which such topics were
perceived, by some, as problematic in their own community. In other
words, the theatre has altered perceptions of what a small town like
Sullivan *should* be like and what one would *expect* to find.

THE LITTLE THEATRE VERSUS *LITTLE THEATRE*

The Little Theatre On The Square has been simultaneously blessed
and cursed. To name a theatre after oneself and have it so well describe almost everything about the operation is more than coinci-
dental. The downside is having the name of the theatre create seri-
ous misconceptions about the *type* of theatre. The Little Theatre On
The Square was founded as a professional, profit-making enterprise,
but because of its name and size, people often believe it to be a traditional "little," or community, theatre.

Community theatres, for most of this century, provided access
to theatre for an entire community as both audience members and
artistic participants. In 1959, there were an estimated thirty-five
hundred full-scale community theatres in the United States producing on a regular basis; that number, according to the American Association of Community Theater, has since doubled. The theatres
range from entirely voluntary enterprises, to those having paid, un-
professional administrative staff members, to those having some mix
of paid professional staff and volunteers.

The distinction between The Little Theatre On The Square and
an ordinary little theatre was, of course, not lost on founder Guy
Little. From the beginning, it was billed as a professional theatre,
combining the talents of veteran performers with college students
and eager amateurs from the area. Little changed the name of his
enterprise from Summer of Musicals to The Little Theatre On The
Square in 1963 when he bought the Grand Theatre. The new name
continued to perpetuate presumptions about the theatre's status
even though in 1959 it had become part of Equity and started featuring easily recognizable stars.

The primary difference between professional and nonprofessional
theatre is affiliation with Actors Equity Association. Actors Equity

is the union that represents actors and stage managers and governs the conditions of their employment. Recent changes in the union and industry have made it easier for an actor to make a living without belonging to Equity, but being a member of Equity and working for a theatre and producer operating under an Equity production contract is the apex of the definition of "professional."

The Actors Equity Association, chartered by the American Federation of Labor in 1913, combined three labor organizations representing actors. Briefly stated, Equity regulates working conditions and sets minimum salaries. Types of Equity contracts have varied over the years, as have membership criteria. Traditionally, young apprentices or interns earned points by working a certain number of weeks under a membership candidacy program before becoming Equity members. Equity also distinguishes between commercial and nonprofit theatres. Currently, Equity has around forty thousand members, but the number does not indicate active employment.

The locus for professional theatre in the United States is New York City, although it extends well beyond Broadway. Professional theatre outside New York generally falls into two categories, regional and summer stock. The focus of regional theatre—also described as resident professional, regional repertory, permanent professional, nonprofit professional, or repertory—is on original productions in major metropolitan areas. Summer stock shares a few similarities with regional theatre. Like regional or repertory theatres, stock theatre uses a core of artistic staff and administrators from production to production. Unlike regional theatre, however, stock theatre is generally found well outside metropolitan areas and can be nonprofessional. Many summer stock theatres, for example, are run by university drama departments.

Until the end of World War II, professional theatre outside New York, as described by Gerald Berkowitz (1982), was limited to summer stock companies "providing unpretentious fare to undiscriminating vacationers" (21). Summer stock evolved during New York theatre's traditionally slow season, with Broadway productions resurfacing in New England and the mid-Atlantic regions, the areas where theatre audiences spent their summer holidays. With limited exception, according to Berkowitz, summer stock seasons were dominated by Broadway hits.

During the 1930s, stock companies, establishing a tradition, produced a twelve-week season, each production usually lasting a week with a visiting star actor featured on the bill. Most of the big stars appeared in only one play all summer, arriving at the theatre just in time for a run-through with the resident cast, playing a week, then moving on to another theatre offering the same play. A variation of this was the entire production being packaged up and sent from theatre to theatre. A more recent variation was featuring, instead of a "Broadway star," anyone who could draw an audience, such as an actor from a soap opera or sitcom.

The Little Theatre On The Square has functioned in many different roles, but its original concept and design were firmly based on the summer stock tradition. Guy Little was a veteran of summer stock on the East Coast and earned his Equity card as a high school student in the early 1950s. The anomaly was where he opened his theatre: *Most* professional summer stock theatres were not in the middle of farming country.

There certainly was professional summer stock in the Midwest, but such theatre typically was either close to a vacation area or in a larger city. The Cherry County Playhouse, an Equity summer stock theatre in Michigan, was closest in concept to The Little Theatre On The Square. Both were founded in the mid- to late 1950s and, in fact, often shared bookings. The primary difference was that the Cherry County Playhouse was originally established in Traverse City, Michigan, a city much larger than Sullivan, Illinois, and a traditional vacation spot along Lake Michigan. The Cherry County Playhouse still produces star theatre but has since moved to Muskegon.

In central Illinois there was no lack of theatre. The University of Illinois in Champaign-Urbana, less than an hour from Sullivan, had (and still has) a notable theatre department. Other colleges and universities in the area also had theatre programs, but, typically, they were located in larger cities and were not inherently professional. The same is true for community theatre. Amateur theatre groups sprang up in cities like Decatur, Mattoon, Champaign, and Peoria; there was even an active community theatre group in Arthur, a town of two thousand people less than twenty miles from Sullivan. These groups were, however, still amateur. Despite the name and lingering assumptions, The Little Theatre On The Square was started as, and has remained, a professional theatre.

From the beginning, Little hired actors, directors, and designers from New York and elsewhere and promoted this fact. Over the course of a very few years and as The Little Theatre became Equity, the focus of attention drifted from some nameless actor, significant only because he or she came from New York, to people who were instantly recognizable. Actors such as Cesar Romero, Joe E. Brown, Margaret Hamilton, Mickey Rooney, and many others cemented The Little Theatre's reputation. It made a small, insignificant farming community in the middle of corn and soybean fields identifiable across the country as "that place with that theatre."

SMALL-TOWN IDEALS AND IMAGES

The story of The Little Theatre On The Square is certainly unusual, but an Equity theatre thriving in a corn town is cause for a cultural double take. Summer stock in the Catskills has a connotation distinctly different from that of summer stock in Moultrie County, primarily because the former fits circumscribed notions of where such a theatre is expected to be. In many ways, professional theatre in a town like Sullivan is as illogical as moving a mountain onto the prairie or building a gothic cathedral to dominate a rural townscape. The unlikely location of the theatre relates directly to an American sense of place and to how perceptions of small-town America are formed.

Sullivan, Illinois, was described by Bella Stumbo in the 30 July 1974 *Los Angeles Times* as "too bland, too utterly wholesome to offer any intrigue whatsoever, merely an enlarged spot in an endlessly flat road, surrounded on all sides by lush cornfields." The same could be said for scores of similar places, but that does not make them all universally known and understood, as Stumbo seems to imply. To some extent, the sentiment of "seen one, seen them all" has an element of truth. A person familiar with Sullivan could easily and genuinely sum up the characteristics of almost any other Midwestern farm town. However, someone who is not accustomed to the nuances of a small town risks classifying *all* small towns as an "enlarged spot" on a road.

Geographic stereotypes are as common, as inaccurate, and as confidently held as any other type of cultural assumption. Peter Gould and Rodney White noted in *Mental Maps* (1986) that ideas about a specific location are reinforced by, among other things, personal narratives and mass-mediated images. These consequently affect expectations one may have about that location. Asking one hundred Americans about Los Angeles, for example, will inspire one hundred different responses about "LA" and what one would expect to experience, ranging from climate to crime. The response is not conditional on whether any had ever visited the city. Asked about other places without such name recognition as Los Angeles, these same hypothetical Americans are likely to respond with culturally stereotyped descriptions based on the idea of a place—a New England village, a college town, an inner city, an affluent suburb—with the same uninformed assurance.

The Midwest does not escape its share of cultural presumptions. At one extreme is the romanticized view of the Midwestern landscape noted by Richard Quinney (1986). He described the transcendent quality of the "line of the horizon, the way the sky meets the land, the drift of the clouds over the fields, the way the sun reflects from the weathered barn" (22). At the other end is the idea that the Midwest is a cityless, cultural void of predictable rectilinear fields—fill dirt between more varied and interesting landscapes, cities, and coasts. In other words, it is an area, noted by John Brinckerhoff Jackson (1994) and Drake Hokanson (1994), best experienced from a jetliner's window.

Such descriptions and accompanying attitudes may partially result from the order these areas had imposed on them well before they were settled. The Land Ordinance of 1785 created a survey grid, establishing everything north of the Ohio River and west of the Pennsylvania-Ohio border into six-mile-square townships. While an efficient system and democratic way of organizing vast amounts of space, an unforeseen consequence of the grid was what Jackson (1994) calls an "all-pervading sameness" (153–55). This system was mandated in areas that were, according to Kent Ryden (1993), "geographically restrained and topographically prudish" and created "a land of compass directions" (290). The regimented character of the landscape creates erroneous assumptions that every other aspect of Midwestern life, especially life in small towns, has similarly platted and predictable features.

The reality of these towns caught in the Midwestern grid lies someplace between the extremes of bucolic idealism and cultural wasteland. Writing specifically about small-town Missouri, Frank Conroy (1993) said, "It may require a certain amount of imagination to move past the faintly patronizing imagery of a Norman Rockwell and get a handle on what it must have felt like to live in one of those towns. Small towns were [and still are] complex social organisms made up of . . . the whole infinite spectrum of human nature" (16–17).

The complexities of small-town life evolve over years and, in some cases, generations of interaction with the same people in the same locations for the same reasons. The everyday patterns of life in places like Sullivan build such a level of familiarity, almost to the point of ritual, that it is often overlooked, especially by outsiders, as simplistic and inconsequential. The geography of an area also plays a role: People interact with the surrounding landscape as they do their neighbors. Residents of an area develop similar intimacies with streetscapes, curves in roads, even the bumps and sounds of railroad crossings. Such habitual contact with people and landscape orders residents' lives and creates and reinforces one's sense of place.

Sense of place in Moultrie County is not developed from a response to majestic landscape or stately architecture. Instead, as John Brinckerhoff Jackson (1994) described, it is created out of familiarity with an area, ritual repetition, and the associated memories. "I am inclined to believe that the average American still associates a sense of place not so much with architecture or a monument . . . as with some event, some daily, weekly, or seasonal occurrence which we look forward to or remember and which we shared with others" (159).

Others share Jackson's idea of an American sense of place. According to Kent Ryden (1993), a sense of place "results gradually and unconsciously from inhabiting a landscape over time, becoming familiar with its physical properties, accruing a history within its confines" (39). David Ames (1995), mirroring Ryden and Jackson's ideas, maintains that place is associated with origin and purpose: Shared space reflects shared ideals and becomes part of the collective consciousness and experience. In other words, such areas are "home."

Other authors suggest Americans come from another tradition. Richard Lingeman (1980), in discussing observations made by Alexis de Tocqueville, notes that instead of a sense of place, the American tradition was—and still is—movement, namely westward migration. This tradition is complemented by a sense of freedom from artificial restraints and feeling of self-determination in being *what* and doing it *where* one chose. Peter Calthorpe (1993) and Terry Pindell (1995) disagree that Americans do not have a sense of place; it is evident, in part, in the traditional small town. Calthorpe and Pindell, however, also agree that Americans have a corresponding sense of movement that creates a sense of placelessness rather than a feeling of freedom or self-determination.

Midwestern small-town America has not escaped late-twentieth-century migration, but in a place like Sullivan, Illinois, most residents have lived there for decades, or their families for generations. A sense of place grows here from shared experiences, giving life a feeling of order and consistency. Lack of size and variety, as previously mentioned, breeds an intense intimacy with one's surroundings, turning the most banal routine into an unconscious ritual. Extended beyond individual experience, such patterns of common activity become sanctioned as the expected norm. This belief, subsequently, is transferred to a town's physical sites, public places that take on almost-sacred meanings.

The idea of public places in small towns becoming sacrosanct holds true in Sullivan. The high school football field, city park, public library are all locations referred to as having a certain implicit reverential quality, depending on the source. The courthouse square and surrounding business district, however, are the sole inviolable spots that encompass everything noble and prosperous about the community.

According to Frank Conroy (1993), every healthy small town had an intangible core, one he equated to a soul. This soul, for Richard Francaviglia (1996), is represented by the small-town American Main Street, which reflects "expressions of collectively shared or experienced assumptions, designs and myths" (xxii). Main Street provides the canvas on which architecture and street plan create a distinctively identifiable and familiar order. As a popular image, Main Street is part of the American collective consciousness and national experience. "On Main Street—according to the shared mythology, at least—the honest merchant, the hardworking townsfolk, and the accessible community government are all found in close proximity to one another. The streetscape reflects what seem to be time-honored traditions nurtured away from cities" (xxiii).

Sullivan's version of this tradition is symbolized by the courthouse square, defined by Francaviglia as a "distinctive American space." The courthouse square is an extension of the dedicated public square, a plot on the grid set aside for public use. As new counties were established, according to Edward T. Price (1986), the courthouse square was usually erected on a new site where it served as the center of the county seat, often the largest town and trade center in the county. The courthouse square, including Sullivan's, was characterized by a "rectangular block surrounded by trees, with the courthouse, often the grandest and most ornate building in the county, standing alone in the middle of the square and the town's leading business houses enclosing the square symmetrically on all four sides" (125).

As made clear in popular culture and real life, the courthouse square is the scene for—in addition to government and commerce—civic gatherings, parades, celebrations, demonstrations, even lynchings, all immediately identifiable images. These events, including a lynching, have all been part of life around the square in Sullivan, Illinois, but another element is part of the scene: Among the businesses surrounding the courthouse is The Little Theatre On The Square.

The theatre as one of many businesses in downtown Sullivan was generally (though not always) understood; it contributed to the prosperity of the city and region. The theatre, however, as an unusual type of employer and cultural attraction often went uncategorized and, therefore, uncomprehended. Activities of employees and patrons were not contained within the confines of the theatre but, instead, spilled outside the front doors. At different times during the day, apprentices relaxed in front and in back of the theatre, and audiences at intermission smoked and stretched their legs in the middle of the street. Consequently, the sight of a dancer using the granite marker honoring Lincoln on the courthouse lawn as a barre to warm up instantly shifted what was expected and presumed to be normal. That kind of incongruity also came to symbolize the inherent contradiction of an Equity theatre in a small Midwestern farming community.

While the image of small-town America does have certain mythic and, therefore, immovable qualities, the realities of life in Sullivan and the history of the theatre are much more yielding. Over the years, the relationship between the theatre and the community has gone through several phases, each with its own legacy, but always returning to the starting point, with community members generally embracing the theatre for what it meant to Sullivan. And despite apparent contradictions, the overriding ideal has been preserved. As Conroy (1993) observed, a town may be small, but the sentiment is "by God, it's our small town" and we wouldn't want it any other way (20).

2

EARLY HISTORY OF SULLIVAN, ILLINOIS, AND THE FIRST SEASON OF THE THEATRE

L ong before Sullivan became known for The Little Theatre, the central part of Illinois was known primarily as part of Lincolniana. Abraham Lincoln traveled through what would become Moultrie County in 1830 and 1831 with his family before settling in southern Coles County, near Charleston. Later, from 1847 to 1857, while practicing law, he rode the Eighth Judicial District Circuit, which included Moultrie County. And, during the 1858 Senate campaign, both Stephen Douglas and Lincoln addressed separate crowds of Sullivan supporters on the same day, almost causing a riot. Lincoln's image is certainly visible, but the implied values that image has come to represent have served as curious juxtaposition to the opening of a professional theatre a century later.

Moultrie County, established in February 1843, was created largely from a section of Shelby County. The first settlers were thirty-five members of the extended Whitley family who migrated from North Carolina and Tennessee to southern Illinois in 1811, moving to what is now Moultrie County in 1826. Described by R. Eden Martin (1996), a Sullivan native turned Chicago attorney and Moultrie County chronicler, "The Whitleys settled on land adjacent to a creek which is still known as Whitley Creek . . . about one quarter mile west of what is now the dividing line between Coles and Moultrie counties" (5, 8).

Sullivan, originally called Asa's Point, was established as the county seat with forty acres and platted with a courthouse square occupying the central block. Sullivan was incorporated as a village in 1850 and as a city in 1872. The population, all white, was 500 in 1850, 528 in 1860, and 742 in 1870. The population jumped to 1,300 in 1873 following the completion in 1870 of two railroads, the Illinois Central and the Toledo and St. Louis.

In his 1983 dissertation on religious leader Samuel Rufus Harshman, Robert William Spriggs described the area from Harshman's memoirs as typical Illinois prairie. Sullivan, in the 1870s and 1880s, had between eleven hundred and twelve hundred people and a railroad connecting the town to Mattoon, fifteen miles to the southeast, and to Decatur, thirty-some miles to the northwest. Sullivan, however, "had no telegraph or industry to speak of except those necessitated by the requirements of a small farming community" (116).

Moultrie County was subdivided into eight townships, which are six-mile-square plats, as determined by the Land Ordinance of 1785. In Illinois, townships are political divisions for county offices and assume certain governmental roles (i.e., roads, care of the indigent, and burial); they have nothing to do with boundaries of cities or villages. According to the 1900 census, Moultrie County had a population of 15,244 with four incorporated villages and one city, Sullivan. Between 1890 and 1900, Sullivan had a more than 60-percent increase in population, growing from 1,468 to 2,399.

At the heart of Sullivan is the present Moultrie County courthouse, built in 1906 on the same site as the two preceding courthouses and the only building in the county listed on the National Register of Historic Places. The courthouse is a three-story classic revival building with four identical sides. It was constructed of Cleveland stone on the first story and red brick on the upper two, along with sandstone columns that support pediments at the roof gables. On top is an octagonal clock tower with a domed copper roof.

Corridors from each entrance lead into a center lobby under the rotunda, dividing the first floor into four equal parts. On the inner walls of the lobby are frescoes of the first two courthouses and pastoral scenes. A series of fifteen framed sketches along the outer walls tells the story of Lincoln in Illinois, something of a "stations of Abraham." The largest print depicts the 1858 Sullivan "debate" with Stephen Douglas.

Each corner of the courthouse lawn has a different memorial or monument. In the southeast corner, there is a badly corroded bronze statue of a Civil War Union soldier, dedicated in 1906. In the southwest corner is a Civil War cannon dedicated in 1907. The barrel of the cannon is a favorite parade viewing spot for children. In the northwest corner is the WCTU fountain, originally dedicated in 1905 and rededicated in 1983. In the northeast corner of the courthouse lawn, across the street from the theatre, is the marble Lincoln Eighth Judicial Circuit Marker with bronze plaque, erected in 1921.

Sullivan's business district surrounds the courthouse on all four sides—with Harrison Street to the north, Main Street to the west, Jefferson Street to the south and Washington Street to the east. The square itself is two blocks southeast of the intersection of Illinois highways 121 and 32, the site of Moultrie County's first (and for decades the only) stoplight.

At the end of the nineteenth century and the beginning of the twentieth, the square witnessed a steady flow of businesses and activities. On the northwest corner of the courthouse lawn, a crowd in 1896 lynched from a tree a man who was imprisoned for assaulting a local woman. Consequently, according to the National Register nomination, all the trees on the square were cut down and have only recently been replaced.

Across the street from where the lynching occurred, at the corner of Main and Harrison, was the Titus Opera House. It was built by a local businessman in 1871, had a seating capacity of eight hundred, and hosted a variety of touring theatre and vaudeville companies, as well as local groups. The opera house burned in 1910 and was replaced on the same spot with the Jefferson Theatre, which was built in 1915 and hosted movies, as well as vaudeville and touring theatre companies. The Jefferson burned in 1924. The Grand Theatre, a movie house, was built in 1928 in the middle of the block on Harrison and showed movies, except during the summers, until the early 1960s. It was leased in 1957 for the first Summer of Musicals and became The Little Theatre On The Square in 1963.

Over the years, Sullivan developed several community institutions and traditions that distinguished it in the area. Sullivan has had continuous newspapers published in town since 1857. As part of its centennial edition, the 5 July 1973 *Moultrie County News* featured detailed histories of its own evolution and that of the *Sullivan Progress,* each covering the area since 1884 and 1869, respectively. Both published weekly papers until the *News* bought the *Progress* in 1979. The two merged in 1981, forming the *News-Progress,* which was published biweekly until 1996, when it returned to weekly publication.

Another distinguishing characteristic is Sullivan's annual Fourth of July celebration and fireworks display, begun in 1922. Described in the 5 July 1973 *Moultrie County News,* the event is held in Wyman Park, named for Albert Wyman, a German-born businessman, who, in 1912, willed money to the city for a forty- to sixty-acre park in the European tradition. Opened at the north end of town in 1915, Wyman Park included a lake for swimming.

From 1930 to 1950, the population of the county remained stable at just over 13,000, but the population of Sullivan grew from 2,339 to 3,470. According to the 1950 census, all but two of the 13,171 people in the county were white.

SULLIVAN BEFORE THE THEATRE

While few people would deny that Sullivan was unique because of the theatre, several people interviewed considered the town to be distinct long before the theatre ever opened. Mamie Palmer, a lifelong resident of Moultrie County and sixty-some–year resident of Sullivan, described the community as always having many advantages, with location and accessibility among the leading distinctions.

Others spoke in more general terms, usually referring to the people in the community. No one, however, could pinpoint a specific trait. Margaret Hollowell, who was born and raised in Sullivan and returned there as an adult, described a cultural awareness, suggesting that Sullivan had more to offer than other towns of comparable size. David Mobley, a businessman who moved to Sullivan in 1961 but grew up in a small farming town in western Illinois, ascribes the cultural awareness to an affluence that is not typical in most agricultural communities. "As there is money, there is the freedom to think and to travel and to realize there is another side to this flat earth."

Whether the perceived openness and awareness were a product

of affluence or something else, the one common element, according to Margaret Hollowell, was the people in the community.

> One of my first memories from childhood is being asked to take a plate out to what were called hobos at that time. We lived on one of the three streets that led to the tracks on the west side of town where the depot was . . . on Monroe Street. I am told now that those who traveled the rails at that time left some kind of mark near houses where they routinely could be fed. I remember I was never allowed to sit on the back porch and talk to them but I was required to take the plate out. Nobody was ever turned away.

Hollowell continued, describing impressions she had while growing up. She grew up on the west side of town, while many of her friends, Guy Little included, lived on the east side. "It always seemed to me as though I lived on the opposite side of town. . . . You could call it the wrong side of town if you wanted to. That wasn't true at all. We all went to the same high school, most of us went to the same church, we all went to camp together . . . so there simply was no economic discrimination."

While the homogeneity may have been reassuring to those on the inside, it presented quite a different view to those on the outside. Newcomers often had a hard time "breaking through," getting rid of an aloofness locals perceived outsiders to have. This was a trait Julio (a.k.a. Jibby) and Ruth Florini noticed on a regular basis as people intermingled in their bar and was something those connected with the theatre faced, especially during the early years. The burden was placed on the newcomers, but it was nothing that, according to Jibby Florini, could not be overcome by extending one's hand and self.

Florini, the son of Italian immigrants and the first Italian of record in Moultrie County, moved to Sullivan in 1941 at the age of twenty-one to open a tavern. When he applied for his liquor license, a special meeting was held to decide whether to approve the application:

> There were . . . twenty or thirty [people] objecting to giving me a license. So the mayor says . . . Doc Miller was his name . . . a real gruff big guy. He said, "I checked Jibby's credentials in Shelbyville." I had been running the place for two or three years; it was a restaurant with beer. "He belongs to the Rotary Club; he pays his bills; he

is a good citizen. He is highly recommended. I see no reason not to give him a license." So the dissenters leave because he is the liquor commissioner and whatever he says goes. So I am writing out this check for five hundred dollars . . . and the mayor says, "Young man, do you know why we had this meeting?" I say, "Yeah, cause I am only twenty-one." And that is what I thought it was. "That is one reason. Main reason is because you are Italian." Just like that. And you know, I didn't lose my cool. I said, "Sir, I am an American of Italian descent." I had never known prejudice until then. I come from Nokomis coal miners . . . Poles, Irish, German . . . all together. I just thought "You old so-and-so, I am going to run the best tavern in the state of Illinois." After I got in there a year, he would bring people through and say, "This is Jibby, and he runs our number one tavern and we are proud to have him." I don't hold grudges. He became one of my best friends. I will never forget that. . . . "That is one reason. Main reason is because you are Italian." That is Sullivan way back . . . 1941.

Jibby Florini was drafted in 1943 and returned to Sullivan and his bar in 1946. His clientele was mainly farmers, workers from the Brown Shoe Company, and members of the softball and bowling teams Florini sponsored. They were, he said, "just ordinary people you'd find in a small town." But when the theatre opened, however, "it transformed this from a little sleepy town to an above-ordinary town. *It* sets us above the rest of the area." The theatre had a similar effect on Jibby's bar partly because of Jibby's own experiences and his willingness to open up to outsiders.

The theatre, according to Sharon White, resident of the community since 1972, made Sullivan. White described the signs on the highways at the edge of town that say "Sullivan, More Than a Small Town." "The theatre, more than anything else," said White, "is why we are more than just an ordinary small town. There is not another little bitty town on the earth that has the kinds of things that go on here."

The influence of the theatre also extended to those people not necessarily associated with it. The influence, according to David Mobley, made the community and the people different; it was—and still is—a source of pride.

People would say "I am from Sullivan" and expect the [other] person to know about the theatre. Not about the school system, not about the land that was worth four thousand dollars an acre but *the* theatre. Even today when I tell people in southern Illinois who can barely read and write that I am a product of Sullivan theatre, I expect them to know. And if they don't, by God, I tell them because I am proud of it.

THE FIRST SEASON

The early history of the theatre has taken on something of an allegoric patina given all the retelling and media attention it received because of its eventual success. The most (mis)quoted article was a 1966 Sunday magazine cover feature in the *St. Louis Globe Democrat,* which called The Little Theatre "The Miracle of Sullivan," but it is often cited as "The Miracle of the Cornfields." Regardless of the version, at the heart is the story of a small-town boy returning home from the big city.

Guy Little returned to Sullivan in the winter of 1957 after graduate study and theatre training in New York and eventually settled in his grandparents' farmhouse with his wife, Jerili, and their two children. From the time he was a five-year-old child in Sullivan, he had wanted to own his own theatre, preferably in central Illinois.

In a 21 July 1966 interview with Robert Best, publisher of the *Moultrie County News,* Jerili Little said she knew a life with Guy would be a life in the theatre. "He was a very exciting and courageous young man to even dream of such a thing." When they started looking for a theatre, she said everything was against them. Her husband had tried to find a theatre in larger area cities, including Champaign and Decatur, before deciding on Sullivan and the Grand Theatre.

According to the legend of the first season, Lee Norton, owner of the Grand Theatre, heard Guy Little was looking for a theatre. In addition to the Grand, Sullivan's only movie house, Norton owned the drive-in theatre, which he had opened in 1952 at the west edge of town. With the drive-in open, Norton had stopped showing movies at the Grand during the summer, making it available for Little.

The prospects, however, for a theatre surviving in Sullivan were slim. "Guy used to come in here and drink schooners of beer," said bar owner Jibby Florini.

He said, "What do you think of me starting a live musical theatre over here?" I said, "What do you mean musical theatre?" He said, ". . . put on musical shows, like Broadway." I said "You are out of your mind. Where are you going to get the people?" And I'll never forget what he said. He said "If you give them a good show at a moderate price . . . they'll come." And I said, "You'll go bankrupt."

Similar skepticism was expressed by others within the community. Marilyn Stubblefield, a Sullivan resident since 1948 and a childhood friend of Little's sister, said most people in town thought the theatre would last the summer and that would be it. But it was not.

Little's theatrical endeavor was originally called the Summer of Musicals, and he produced nine musicals in as many weeks. The season's total attendance, according to a tenth-anniversary feature in the 21 July 1966 *Moultrie County News,* was eighty-five hundred. Each show ran four performances, Thursday through Sunday, with, according to Little, "relatively decent audiences." Ticket prices ranged from $.90 to $2.20. *Guys and Dolls,* the final production, sold out, and the balcony was opened for extra seating. That was the first indication there would be a second season.

A 21 June 1957 story in the *Moultrie County News* described the alterations necessary to make the movie house suitable for musicals. Little removed the first four rows of seats to enlarge the stage. The size of the stage subsequently was twenty-seven feet wide and seventeen feet deep with apron, with a proscenium that was seventeen feet high. Little used gallon paint cans painted black for light cans, all controlled with a single dimmer. The theatre, which had no wing or fly space, also had no dressing room space. Cast members had to change in the alley in back of the theatre or use the basement of Dr. Philip Best's office across the street and half a block up from the stage door entrance. Seating capacity on the main floor was 409; except for the last two performances of the season, the balcony was never used.

From the beginning, the Summer of Musicals was billed as the area's only professional theatre, even though it was not considered legitimate by union standards. Little, a member of Actors Equity Association since 1951, used Equity actors during the first season, but the theatre did not officially become a legitimate Equity theatre until 1959. Little drew on his own theatre experience in summer stock and New York to bring in actors. Little also brought in the choreographer and music director from New York.

In addition, Little relied heavily on people from the community and surrounding area, including friends and family members. Marilyn Stubblefield and her husband, Bill, who owned a local car dealership, were among those who helped out during that first season. Bill built sets while his wife sold tickets and did her bit in front of the curtain.

> Guy's sister and I, we had one line. Well it was this little sing-song deal. . . . I don't even remember the story of the *Song of Norway* . . . we were the owners of a conservatory. . . .
>
> This is a momentous moment for our dear conservatory.
> Those who have hissed us now will list us in another category.
> That's our whole thing in the show. I was very nervous about it. Guy's mother was in a lot of shows . . . and his sister Ellen's husband. So there was a lot of catch-as-catch-can that first year.

The theatre really became a Little family venture. Little and his wife (and eventually his children) worked in any artistic or technical capacity in which they were needed, and his parents oversaw the business end. His mother, Inis, had been a high school English teacher and had directed plays at the school. His father, Guy Sr., was a farm manager and landowner. They both wound up working for him as the theatre took shape, his mother running the box office and his father working as business manager.

Brigadoon

As a narrative, the first season of The Little Theatre has a mythic quality: a hometown boy returning from the big city to see his dreams realized, all the while surrounded by supportive friends and family. The significance of the event, however, goes much beyond a modern folktale with a happy ending. The theatre forever changed the way in which Sullivan would be perceived.

When *Brigadoon* opened on 3 July 1957, it opened in something of a Brigadoon. Sullivan was a culturally isolated farming community with a population, according to the 1950 census, of 3,470, all of whom were white. What occurred in Sullivan was more than just a small-town (yet still professional) revival of a ten-year-old musical. The town had its initial introduction to "theatre people," which was a bigger shock and would have a much more lasting effect than any given production would ever have.

The first production met, as did the whole theatre venture, with generally positive reactions. The *Moultrie County News* did not review the first production as such but, in a 12 July 1957 article, did describe it in terms of "an excellent crowd" attending the premiere performance. Little said he was pleased with the performance and cast, "and I can be very critical."

Robert Gwaltney, an Equity actor and veteran of scores of Little Theatre productions including the first, remembered opening night a bit more prosaically. In the 18 September 1966 *Globe-Democrat* feature, Gwaltney recalled standing in front of the theatre at curtain time in kilts and Scottish costumes wondering whether anyone would show up. He said about seventy-five did.

Audience attendance did not significantly improve after that opening night. The rest of the first season's productions—with one notable exception—also met with limited success. The choice of musical, and later drama, was rarely consequential; what was exceptional was that The Little Theatre was a professional enterprise. The novelty aspect of the theatre in Sullivan, at least in the beginning, was magnified by the mix of professional and amateur performers. This mix was, in fact, the focus of a full-page photo feature entitled "Professional, Amateur Actors Combine to Give Sullivan Musical Series" in the 4 July 1957 *Decatur Herald and Review*. The newspaper served a sizable portion of central Illinois, including the areas where several of the amateur actors came from.

Amateur talent, with very limited exception, was used only during the first couple of years. The consequence of the theatre in Sullivan as it evolved and grew over the years was the people it brought into town. The "theatre people" who came to town generally fell into two categories, the stars and everybody else. The stars tended to be well known and easily recognizable, and the surprise, for the most part, was how normal they were. The bulk of people associated with the theatre were the secondary Equity players, the apprentices, and the techies, those behind the scenes. It was this group who, on one hand, tended to be more a part of the community but, on the other, were distinct from area residents. As Joe Florini, Jibby

Florini's son, observed, "Theatre people have their own ways of do-ing things . . . in terms of the way they fit into society. They brought an element of the city to a small community that, at that time, was not prepared to totally accept it." It was also this group who were called "showdogs," a word that has lingered in one variation or another. In 1957, however, Sullivanites were getting only their first taste of theatre people and "showdog" had yet to become part of the vernacular.

The Summer of Musicals was first announced in the *Moultrie County News* on 3 May 1957. According to the news story, Little cast the lead roles in New York in early May and returned to Sullivan in time for the local auditions scheduled at the end of the month. Cast as Tommy Albright, the leading man for *Brigadoon,* was Ron Rogers, an Equity actor and baritone from New York who became a familiar face around Sullivan over the next fifteen years. Also cast for lead roles were Greg Barry, Maureen Reidy, and Jerili Little, all of whom appeared in most, if not all, of the season's productions.

The people cast in supporting and chorus roles were usually those garnered from local auditions. Many were high school and college students from the area, including the son of the county state's at-torney and daughter of a Sullivan physician. Among the area par-ticipants were also Jean Florini (née Hudson) of Bethany and Joe Florini of Sullivan.

The announcement for local auditions attracted the attention of Jean Florini's grandmother who encouraged Jean, a high school junior, to give it a try. The desire to have fun won out over her ini-tial reluctance, and she got a spot. Auditions for men and women were held on subsequent days, and once the roles were cast, couples were paired up and the dances were blocked. Each girl was assigned a boy as a dance partner. Jean Florini remembered, "They said, 'Joe Florini,' and I had never heard of an Italian name and I thought, 'You might know I'd get stuck with some crud.' But when I saw him, I was thrilled. And then I got stuck with that name permanently."

Jean Florini said the summer at the theatre was great fun, but she also found it to be an eye-opening experience in many regards, including being made aware of the establishment run by her future father-in-law. "[Bethany] was dry, and my mother and grandmother had never been in a tavern before. I always thought Jibby was a woman and it was a sinful place, that tavern. And then I found out that it was his parents' [place] and . . . I realized they had a pretty neat son."

The job at the theatre proved to be as educational. Rehearsals often went until two A.M., and while Florini could drive, parents wouldn't let their children, especially girls, stay out that late.

> My mother would come and sit on the streets with a couple of mothers and they would just sit there and talk and wait on us until early morning hours and take us home. We'd come back and practice the next day. . . . I loved it. I thought it was great fun. It was work and—especially when you were just sixteen and a little farm girl and hadn't been around—it opened your eyes to a lot of other things. The energy and excitement I liked, but . . . I was shocked. I was surprised at how volatile everyone's temper was. They were very creative people, and I think they expressed that in their feelings and I wasn't used to that. . . . Chairs would fly.

Putting it into perspective, Florini realized many of the actors were just kids themselves and under much pressure to make the theatre work. They were not paid, did not really have a place to live, and would just be getting off work when the rest of the community was sound asleep.

Jibby Florini, owner of Jibby's tavern, did, in many ways, realize the pressure the theatre folks were under. As the first Italian of record in Moultrie County, he knew what it was like to be an outsider and, as a result, extended his hospitality. He also extended his son, Joe.

Looking back, Joe Florini, who as a high school student was in the chorus of the first show, considered the opening of the theatre to be a great cultural shock with limited prospects for it either making a go or being accepted by the community. "They had a hard time because of the hours they kept . . . of even finding a place to eat. There weren't any fast food places. The [only] places open when they got finished were the taverns, and Dad served food, unlike some of the others. And of course he got involved with feeding them." This involvement, combined with a desire to sing and a lack of acceptable alternative ways to spend the summer, led to the younger Florini's short career in show business. "What else are you to do when you are a sophomore in high school and not old enough to drive? It sounded like fun, and, at that age, we couldn't do anything anyway. Making money was putting up hay and cutting weeds out of beans and detasseling corn for fifty or seventy-five cents an hour. But this was a lot more work than any of those—a lot more work."

Joe Florini lasted for one show. In addition to performing, building sets, and anything else in the theatre, cast members also had to sell tickets, which consisted of hawking them around the square and going through the bleachers at the park during the Fourth of July festivities trying to get people to see the show. At that point, Florini said, "the toughest thing that would have been on me would be in sports with the coach. These people were meaner than the coach. . . ." After Joe's brief career in the theatre, he said he spent a lot of time with Jean's mother and grandmother out in the car "visiting . . . and politicking because I didn't have anything else to do at night. There wasn't any movie theatre. That was the theatre. It was being used."

The stage careers of the Florinis may have been brief but were in no way the end of their relationship with the theatre or each other. Jean Florini lasted the summer but did not seek a second season. She and Joe were married after college and returned to Sullivan after Joe graduated from law school. Jibby and Ruth continued to extend their hospitality to the theatre folks, and Jibby's became the place for audience members to go after the performance. Known as the "Sardi's of Sullivan," Jibby's business expanded threefold. He put the theatre production stills of the stars on the walls, expanded his menu from cheese sandwiches to pizza to steaks, and made everybody welcome.

Jibby's desire to make the theatre people welcome, along with his sense of business and decency, had a lingering effect in the community that spread beyond the realm of the theatre. Even though Sullivan was not dry, the taverns were considered to be workingmen's (i.e., blue-collar) establishments. And with the exception of the country club, there were no reputable places to consume alcohol. A person had to go out of town, drink at home, or not at all. As will be shown, the theatre and Jibby's played a distinct role in altering perceptions of taverns and who would be seen in one.

THIS COULD BE THE START OF SOMETHING BIG

The success of *Guys and Dolls*, the final production of the first season, provided the needed incentive to think about a second season. But what allowed the theatre to survive was more than just a well-attended final show. It was a combination of several related factors, including much good fortune and chutzpah.

The story of the creation of the theatre centered on Little's childhood dream and his returning to his hometown to make it come true. Few would deny Little was blessed with an uncharacteristic determination and drive. These were combined with charm, intelligence, amazing resourcefulness, and an inexhaustible perseverance. When people were telling him a successful theatre in such a small town was impossible, he responded that not only could it be done but that he would be the one to do it.

Even with his collection of personal attributes, he still had the home court advantage, surrounded as he was by supportive friends and family members. It is generally agreed that an outsider could not have made it work. Joe Florini mirrors sentiments of several people interviewed: "It's a combination, a total package. He [Guy] had to have the monetary support; he had to have the support of his wife, his parents, and their respectability. . . . Jerili was crucial to its success." She was the female lead in productions during the first season and continued in a variety of functions, including directing.

Little's parents also played key roles. It was already noted that his mother took over the box office and his father ran the business end of things. Both also ushered, and his mother, a high school English and drama teacher, appeared on stage in several roles. Her most noteworthy role, according to local memories, was as Joe E. Brown's aunt in *Harvey*. And while such activity may not seem incongruous for parents supporting their son's activity, they also had a reputation of social and financial prominence within the community that showing ticket holders to their seats did not quite match.

The role Little's family played, especially as financial supporters, set a precedent for how the theatre was run. This family involvement, in turn, gave rise to mistaken community assumptions about how the theatre was or should be financed. Such false impressions have lasted the theatre's entire history. Even after Little no longer had any professional association with the theatre—except for the name on the marquee—it was believed the theatre was still a Little family enterprise, well sponsored by family money. In the beginning, however, the theatre was essentially a family business which, in part, is what enabled it to continue beyond the first season.

On stage July 3 – 8
MARK RYDELL
GLASS MENAGERIE

From 1957 to 1962, Guy S. Little Jr. rented the Grand Theatre. He bought it in 1963 and changed the name to The Little Theatre On The Square. (Courtesy David W. Mobley)

Photographed in the early 1960s, the Moultrie County Courthouse has essentially remained unchanged since it was built in 1904. (Courtesy David W. Mobley)

Audience members seek autographs from Mark Rydell, star of *The Glass Menagerie,* in the alley behind the theatre in 1962. (Courtesy David W. Mobley)

Peter Palmer first appeared at The Little Theatre in 1962. (Courtesy David W. Mobley)

Ann B. Davis starred in *Everybody Loves Opal* in 1963. (Courtesy David W. Mobley)

Margaret Truman appeared with Ron Rogers in *Late Love* in 1963. (Courtesy David W. Mobley)

Inis Little, mother of Guy S. Little Jr., appeared in several productions, including *Harvey* with Joe E. Brown in 1963. (Courtesy David W. Mobley)

Linda Darnell died in a fire in the Chicago area shortly after appearing in *Janus* in Sullivan in 1964. (Courtesy David W. Mobley)

John Carradine, who starred in *Dracula* in 1965 and in *Oliver* in 1966, was known to recite Shakespeare at Jibby's Tavern. (Courtesy David W. Mobley)

Rosemary Prinz appeared at the theatre more than any other star. She did *Mary, Mary* in 1965. (Courtesy David W. Mobley)

Guy S. Little Jr. *(second from left)* included his daughter, Vanessa *(third from right)*, and son, Sean *(far right)*, in a production of *Carousel* in 1966. (Courtesy David W. Mobley)

Jerili Little, then married to Guy S. Little Jr., was an integral part of many productions. She starred with Dennis Weaver in *Catch Me If You Can* in 1966. (Courtesy David W. Mobley)

Peter Palmer, with Senator Charles Percy *(left)*, announced his engagement to Aniko Farrell *(right)* in Sullivan in 1966. (Courtesy David W. Mobley)

Guy S. Little Jr. during a rehearsal in 1967. (Courtesy David W. Mobley)

Mercedes McCambridge starred in *Who's Afraid of Virginia Woolf?* in 1967. The dog was a gift from Adlai Stevenson. (Courtesy David W. Mobley)

Rosemary Prinz, an audience favorite, signed autographs for her fans in the theatre house in 1967. (Courtesy David W. Mobley)

Pat and Eloise O'Brien appeared in Sullivan six times between 1963 and 1972. This photograph was used for the playbill cover of *Holiday for Lovers* in 1969. (Courtesy David W. Mobley)

3

THEATRE IN THE CORNFIELDS

—⸺⸨⸩⸺—

The 1958 season in many ways resembled the theatre's first year. The majority of support, financial and artistic, came from family and friends, and Guy S. Little Jr. again relied on local talent with a number of featured performers from the first season returning for a second year. Little added one musical, doing ten productions in ten weeks, each running Wednesday to Sunday. The two major differences in the second year were the addition of air conditioning and a dramatic increase in audience attendance. According to the 21 July 1966 *Moultrie County News,* the audience attendance for the second season more than doubled, drawing 17,900, and, as if repeating the pattern from the first season, the second season's final production, *Oklahoma!,* peaked that summer's attendance with the final six performances attracting 3,000 people.

The third season marked a dramatic shift in the direction of the theatre. For the first time, each of the ten musicals ran for a week with each Monday dark. More important, 1959 was the year The Little Theatre became an Equity house and featured its first "star." While Little had used Equity actors during the first and second seasons, he also used many non-Equity performers and could not afford to meet the demands the union made—the number of Equity actors required for each production, pay scale, et cetera. In 1959, however, Little was able to work with Equity to adapt the union requirements to the unique circumstances at The Little Theatre On The Square, making it the first and only Equity theatre between Chicago and St. Louis.

At the same time, Little featured an actor with immediate name recognition, Annamary Dickey, in *Song of Norway*. Dickey made her debut with the Metropolitan Opera in 1939 and made the leap to Broadway where she appeared in several musicals including *Allegro* in 1947, a musical in which she also appeared at The Little Theatre in 1966. More important, she was also from Decatur and had attended Millikin University.

Annamary Dickey's relative celebrity and association with central Illinois established a precedent: Decatur-area residents came to see Dickey rather than to specifically see *Song of Norway* or the theatre. This set the pattern for theatergoers of The Little Theatre for the next twenty years. Audiences, by and large, were attracted to come and see a specific star; the play he or she was in was often irrelevant. Sharon White, a part of the theatre since 1973, said people would not call up and ask what show was playing. "They would say, 'Who is playing at the theatre?' They didn't ask what the show was; they asked what the name of the star was. They came to see not *Born Yesterday*, they came to see Betty Grable. They didn't come to see *Li'l Abner*, they came to see Peter Palmer. They came to see a star."

This practice would get a slight twist when Little began hiring actors from soap operas the following season, although Little continued to engage stars from Broadway and Hollywood. During the 1960 season, he featured, among others, Ruth Warrick, Margaret Hamilton, and a young Alan Alda. It was Ruth Warrick who started the long line of actors from soap operas appearing in Sullivan. Consequently, instead of inquiring at the box office about an actor by name, audience members would just ask to see the show in which a specific soap opera character was appearing.

In 1960, when she appeared at The Little Theatre in *Pal Joey*, Ruth Warrick played Aunt Edie in *As the World Turns*, a role she had held since 1955. (Warrick subsequently became Aunt Phoebe on *All My Children*, a role she has held since 1970.) In a 6 May 1991 interview with the *News-Progress*, Guy Little said he had never followed soap operas and had no idea who Aunt Edie was. He knew Warrick had been a major movie star in the 1930s and had starred in 1941 as Orson Welles's wife in *Citizen Kane*. "Her main draw to our [theatre] audiences, however, was the soap opera role."

Little, continuing to reminisce about engaging soap opera stars in the 1991 interview, said that after Warrick's success, audience members approached him, saying "Oh, we loved Aunt Edie but get Penny." Little recalled not knowing Penny from a copper coin. Penny, in fact, turned out to be Rosemary Prinz, also from *As the World Turns,* and who returned to The Little Theatre more times than any other star. She also helped to cement the theatre's reputation financially and artistically. Prinz auditioned for Little to do *Paint Your Wagon* for the 1961 season. She was, as Little described, "an absolute sensation." Little explained how Prinz really had no idea how popular she would be. She even brought her mother so she would have at least one person in the audience. Prinz wound up attracting record crowds. For weeks, the box office would get calls about the "Penny Show."

Rosemary Prinz was the best example of audiences being drawn to a soap opera character rather than an individual artist's own name. Even though Prinz returned to Sullivan year after year, people still wanted to see "Penny" and often referred to her that way. Little took advantage of this, said Sharon White, and focused the publicity that way. Advertisements would, for example, say "Come see Penny in . . ." whatever show in which Prinz was appearing. "And it worked. It built the theatre."

Margaret Hollowell mirrors White's sentiments of what Rosemary Prinz did for the theatre. "She was the one who turned it around and made it profitable because she was so hot on television. Fans started coming by the bus and truckload. There would be these lines in the alley afterward. Everybody would just nearly smother her wanting autographs, wanting to tell her how much she changed their lives."

Marketing actors on the basis of their appeal on daytime television was a relatively new phenomenon, because the audience of soap operas and related marketing was women. And, as Sharon White observed, women were also the driving force in the theatre audiences. "The women are the ones who get the groups together to come down here. The women are the ones who buy the tickets and say 'Come on, honey. We are going to the show.'"

Eileen Fulton, Lisa on *As the World Turns,* appeared at The Little Theatre a half dozen times. She described in her 1970 autobiography how, in 1964 after leaving the soap opera and being replaced by another actor, fans and the media wondered, "Where is the real Lisa?" The theatre in Traverse City, Michigan, where she was appearing in *Grand Prize,* answered the question: "Lisa is at the Cherry County Playhouse" (166–67).

The trend of hiring actors from soap operas continued throughout the tenure of the star system at The Little Theatre. Of those who came from daytime television, the majority of actors came from the same program, *As the World Turns.* Most came to Sullivan with stage experience. This, combined with their successes on the small screen, generally made for memorable and good productions. Toward the middle to late 1970s, star theatre was getting expensive and the pickings were becoming slim. Among the actors small theatres like The Little Theatre could afford, few had stage experience or any lasting name recognition. They, consequently, were easily forgotten and slipped into oblivion. But, as Sharon White pointed out, when an actor appeared in Sullivan and had top billing, it meant that person was hot and a star.

THE THEATRE AND THE COMMUNITY

As The Little Theatre On The Square started to have the first inklings of success, and as the area's only professional theatre, it naturally drew attention to itself and the community. Guy Little advertised throughout the area and was a firm believer in the benefits of spreading the news by word of mouth. Similarly, the effect of the theatre within the community became a familiar topic in newspaper editorials. But, despite the attention and growing numbers of people coming to the theatre, Sullivan, Illinois, was still a small farming town with fewer than four thousand people and only one stoplight.

After the theatre's successful first season, the rhetoric of "good for the theatre, good for Sullivan" began to circulate. In an editorial in the 19 June 1958 *Moultrie County News,* the issue in which the first production of the season was announced, publisher Louise Lippincott predicted a "banner season" and said attending the theatre meant also "supporting a project that has brought much favorable publicity to Sullivan and is bound to bring much more." Lippincott also pointed out the distinction between theatre and other forms of entertainment, a distinction that would continue to be made for decades to come. "For the uninitiated, a live production of a musical can't be topped for entertainment. There's none of the dullness, interference, or commercials that are earmarks of black-and-white television and there's none of the flatness and faraway feeling that you get from movies. You are there in a live production and almost feel a part of the show."

The city, too, became part of the act when Sullivan's mayor, Ivan "Cotton" Wood, declared 30 June 1960 to be Summer of Musicals Day. As recalled in the 21 July 1966 *Moultrie County News,* the mayor proclaimed the theatre the "city's outstanding summer drawing attraction . . . and a renowned point of identification." Other events included Guy Little speaking on the background of the musical shows over coffee at the Candyland Cafe and giving residents a glimpse behind the scenes of *South Pacific,* the season's first production.

Sullivan residents were also made a part of the larger show as the effects of the theatre began to be felt within the community. Just as Little relied on the kindness of friends and family for what occurred on stage, he drew people into the expanding influence of his blooming enterprise. And just as involving local people in the first couple of seasons made the theatre identifiable, including residents in the associated activities had an equally tangible result.

Sullivan, especially in the early 1960s, was never mistaken for a tourist destination. Needless to say, guest accommodations for the visiting stars were nonexistent. There were no real restaurants—Jibby's, then, was just a tavern with a hospitable owner who served food—or hotels. This lack of accommodations, especially the lack of hotels, became a problem as bigger and brighter stars came to town. Fortunately, Little was able to solve that problem and address a second issue, community relations, at the same time.

When the theatre first opened, featured players had to stay in hotels in either Mattoon or Decatur, twenty and thirty miles from Sullivan, respectively, and they either had to drive themselves or have someone drive them back and forth. In 1960, when the idea of headlining stars appeared to be working, Little wanted someplace close for them to stay. He asked Mamie Palmer, a friend of his mother, and her husband, Art, the county coroner, to house the stars that summer. The idea, said Mamie Palmer, was if she and her husband did it, other people would take in actors as well, especially the supporting actors. Their house, consequently, became nicknamed "the Sullivan Palmer House" after the Chicago hotel, and local folklore has it more than one star was shocked to discover they weren't staying at the real Palmer House.

The Palmers lived barely a block and a half north of the stage door entrance in an early-twentieth-century, two-story, white frame house with a substantial and secluded garden. Often, the actors used the Palmer House as a dressing room during intermission. During the summer, the Palmers turned the downstairs, with two bedrooms and a bath, over to the actors while the Palmers lived on the second floor. They usually hosted two at a time; often one would be performing while the other would be in rehearsal. Mamie Palmer said the actors made themselves at home, came and went as they pleased, made their own coffee, and often made their own beds. Their schedules with performances were such that often the Palmers would go two or three days without seeing their guests.

The first stars to stay with the Palmers were Ruth Warrick, performing in *Pal Joey,* and Margaret Hamilton, rehearsing *A Tree Grows in Brooklyn,* the following show. One evening after midnight, according to an often-told story, the old Gauger Lumber Yard, a block south of the square, caught on fire and Warrick joined a crowd of Sullivanites to watch it burn. Little wandered down to watch as well and found Warrick manning a fire hose, along with the volunteer fire fighters. Around two A.M., when Little escorted Warrick back to the Palmer House, she realized she was locked out. Not wanting to wake anyone, she told Little to crawl into a window and open the front door. Little crawled through a bedroom window only to wake Margaret Hamilton who said, "Guy, dear, what are you doing in my room"?

"When Guy quit having the stars, I quit . . . as much as I enjoyed them," said Palmer. "I did it for a long time so I am taking life easy now." Now in her nineties, Mamie "taking life easy" is still busier than many people half her age. She still stays in touch with a number of her former guests, the ones who stayed with her the most often. Rosemary Prinz and Peter and Aniko Palmer occasionally return to Sullivan to help her celebrate her birthdays.

Little kept a variety of actors himself at his family's redone farmhouse south of town, but his getting people to host the stars did bring about the desired results. Not only did others take in actors, other people around Sullivan started to see how "normal" the stars were. This realization, as described by Jean Florini, affirmed what was becoming a collective view within the community about the theatre. "Some people were shocked to see that those people [the stars] were really normal people . . . working really hard at what they did," said Florini. "They loved coming to a little community and saying 'Oh, it's so nice to be able to relax and people are so sweet to us and we don't have to lock our cars and everyone is so trusting.' Most people, I think, found them friendly. It worked both ways."

Another aspect of having a professional theatre in town was the opening and closing night parties. This activity also drew community members into the fold of the theatre. The people who took in actors and hosted parties were those who were already attracted to the theatre. There were exceptions, but for the most part, those who were part of the theatre's social scene were already among the converted.

One person who has played—and continues to play—a major part in the theatre's role in the community is Margaret Hollowell (then Barlow). A childhood friend of Little, she returned to Sullivan in the fall of 1960 with her family, moved into her grandmother's huge and vacant house toward the center of town, and took a job as speech pathologist with the school district. The way she got involved with, as she describes it, the "theatre generation" was by hosting the opening night party for Margaret Truman, who appeared in *Late Love* in 1963 with Ron Rogers.

Rogers was already staying with Hollowell and her family. "You have undoubtedly heard that we didn't have any motels at that time . . . not [where] you would put anybody. Those of us who had extra space kept them in our homes. I had a downstairs bedroom with its own bath. That was an ideal place, and they could come and go as they chose."

This system generally worked, although there were notable exceptions. Margaret Truman did not want to intrude on anyone, nor did she want to stay out of town. This, according to an often-repeated story, left one option, the Hotel Milroy, otherwise known as the "Hotel Mildew." Little said Truman was perfectly content at the Milroy but described how she had to go down an alley strewn with old tires and paint cans and whatever else to get to her room.

Little said he always wanted a photograph of Truman at the Milroy with the caption "The White House never looked like this."

In addition to housing the male lead, Margaret Hollowell's role also extended to hosting the opening night party. Little's wife, Jerili, was directing *Late Love,* was rehearsing for the next show, *Carnival,* and was, as Hollowell put it, "at her wit's end." Hollowell volunteered to host the party since she was already going to be there. She figured, because the play was only a two- or three-character show and that there was a minimal technical staff, the party would not be too large. "There was no costumer as such. Guy did the costumes then, and the men just wore their own clothes."

When Hollowell asked what to serve, Jerili instructed her to call Mrs. Switzer who would figure out something.

> Mrs. Switzer was the institution who cooked for us for these gigantic parties. Sometimes we would have sixty, seventy people because press would show up, and if you had a big cast . . . if you had twenty or thirty in the cast, plus press plus some of the rest of us, it got to be a lot of people. It wasn't that I didn't have the room, it's just that you never wanted to run out of food, if you could avoid it.

For a small party, like the one for Margaret Truman, Hollowell said, usually, a casserole, a salad, maybe fruit or something was plenty.

> We got it together and they wound up singing in the living room to records, and Miss Truman sat in my son's antique wicker rocker. . . . I knew it wasn't very well put together, and I prayed that she wouldn't fall through to the floor and we would not be able to get her out. She and Ron Rogers sang until about three in the morning. It was such fun.

Hollowell also described another party that had a different kind of hitch. Dennis Weaver appeared in 1966 in *Catch Me If You Can,* and Hollowell again threw the opening night party. And while adapting to special diets, especially a vegetarian one, might be common practice now, thirty years ago it muddled more than one host.

> It was just hotter than the hinges of hell . . . but if you could keep enough fans going, and by eleven o'clock at night . . . it wasn't too ungodly uncomfortable. We had arranged at the country club to do an entrée salad with crabmeat . . . and found out the morning of the opening night that he was a vegetarian. I called Jack [the chef at

the country club] in a panic and he said "that's okay. We'll just have avocado salad." So he made the avocados the rich part of the salad, and it worked out fine. [Weaver] didn't drink anything but orange juice. He was really big on television at that time . . . and I had the feeling he kind of wondered what the hell he was doing out in the cornfields.

Jibby Florini had a bit of an easier time. "[Weaver] would always come in and say, 'Give me one of those vegetable pies.' That's a pizza without meat."

SHOW TIME IN THE CORNFIELDS

By the early 1960s, the theatre was firmly situated on the track it would take for the next several years. It became Equity in 1959, started hiring actors with easily recognizable names and faces, had tapped into the soap opera star market, which would put butter on its bread, and had been acknowledged by the city as an "identifying characteristic." The theatre had already begun creeping into the social fabric of the community by involving certain residents with, literally, the care and feeding of the stars. This tradition, in part, perpetuated ideas of how "normal" the stars were, especially among those community residents not associated with the theatre.

The Little Theatre had also established a familiar pattern of events that surrounded each production, events such as rehearsals, opening nights, and press conferences. These drew a wide variety of businesses and individuals into the theatre's seasonal rituals. On one hand, the theatre was simply a local business located on Sullivan's square and thus interacted with other area businesses and individuals during the busy summer season. On the other hand, individuals viewed the theatre as a unique attraction and intentionally relocated businesses into the community. Scattered throughout was a mix of people who found themselves in Sullivan for reasons indirectly related to the theatre but played very active parts in the theatre's events. For these people, the theatre provided opportunities they may otherwise never have found and, for many, the theatre became a fundamental and lasting part of their lives.

Any given season at The Little Theatre On The Square was planned during the preceding season. According to a 25 June 1959 *Moultrie County News* article, Guy Little selected cast members from auditions in New York and Chicago during the off-season. He averaged thirty-five performers for each production, a mix of new people gleaned from auditions and those who had appeared in Sullivan the previous season.

While, to Sullivan audiences, there might have seemed to be an abundance of available musicals and, later, dramas from which to choose, Little had his challenge cut out for him. Over the years, Little often noted the difficulty in finding "wholesome plays with wholesome stars" that appealed to Midwestern audiences. In a 21 July 1966 interview with Wayne Allen for the *Moultrie County News,* Little noted a geographic distinction to theatre tastes. "The glamorous sexy stars who go over big in the East and on the West Coast have not been successful here." Instead, Little looked for stars with "down-to-earth images," which he said his audiences preferred.

The demand for wholesomeness even extended to the star's behavior off the stage, as Eileen Fulton noted in her updated, 1995 autobiography. Fulton appeared in Neil Simon's *The Star Spangled Girl* in the fall of 1970. "Sullivan loved me," Fulton wrote, at least until Danny Fortunato, her swarthy record producer–lover showed up. "I had been there before, and they always looked upon me fondly, as if I were their little girl. The good people of Sullivan perceived that this dark stranger was soiling their princess." Fulton continued that her little scandal did not hurt business in the least. People who would no longer say hello as she walked down the street holding hands with Danny packed the theatre every night to see "this 'bad' woman" on stage in a light-hearted comedy" (98).

Each show generally ran for two weeks, though there certainly were exceptions. Sometimes, especially in the 1960s, to get a specific star in Sullivan for a desired length of time, it was necessary to book the actor for a month or more and share the booking with other theatres. Little often booked the same star and show with theatres in Michigan and Ohio and moved the actor from one theatre to another. Usually, only the star would change theatres and would often have a very short time to rehearse with the resident company and get used to a different stage. When actors would go from the Cherry County Playhouse in Michigan to The Little Theatre or vice versa, they would move between a tent theatre on a parking lot of a hotel to a proscenium stage in an old movie house.

Little added nonmusicals to the theatre's repertoire in 1962 with *The Tunnel of Love* with Eddie Bracken and *The Glass Menagerie* with Mark Rydell, who was also from *As the World Turns*. For both musicals and nonmusicals, he maintained the practice of a familiar name in an unfamiliar play and vice versa. Sometimes, if he wanted a specific star, it meant producing the show that actor was in. For instance, when Little hired Cesar Romero, it meant booking *Strictly Dishonorable*, the only show Romero did. On the other hand, if a show had just been released to stock, Little said he would try to find a familiar face. Andy Devine, who came back several times, was a last-minute replacement for Richard Deacon in *Never Too Late*.

The Little Theatre never did any original productions, but it did try out new shows before they began to tour. These included *Timid Tiger* with John Payne and *Goodbye, Ghost* with June Allyson. The Little Theatre also premiered two shows with Eve Arden, *The Most Marvelous News* and *Under Papa's Picture,* with memorable success in Sullivan and later on tour.

As the decade progressed, the pattern for the theatre's activities became more practiced, more refined. Each show opened on a Tuesday night. The star usually came into town a week early to rehearse with the resident company, which was already performing in a currently running show. Immediately after the star arrived in Sullivan, David Mobley, the theatre's photographer, would shoot something to be used in front of the theatre and on the cover of the playbill. Publicity shots were usually done during the dress rehearsal. He would then process the film and print immediately to include a couple of stills in the press packets sent to media outlets around the area.

As previously mentioned, Guy Little relied heavily on spreading the message of the theatre via word of mouth. This, of course, did not preclude other types of advertising. Lee York, who did public relations for the theatre from 1963 to 1968, described releases being sent to newspapers and radio and television stations in an area that spread from Gilman, Illinois, to Effingham to Jacksonville to Terre Haute, Indiana. "At the beginning of each season," said York, "we also sent complimentary press passes good for opening night when the request for tickets was accompanied by a tear sheet about the show."

News of a current production and featured star was also spread through interviews with the star. Jane Krows, a stringer of sorts for a Decatur newspaper, regularly interviewed stars from her home for a radio spot for an area radio station. York said a few stars were interviewed in Sullivan by visiting reviewers, but primarily he recalled driving the stars to various area cities. Mobley, too, played chauffeur, but of a different sort. Licensed for single-engine aircraft, Mobley said he occasionally would fly the star to Peoria or St. Louis for television or radio interviews.

The theatre was for Mobley and York, as it was for many others, an outlet for creative energy they otherwise would not have found in a town of four thousand people. Before taking on the theatre's public relations full-time in 1965, York had been the band director at Sullivan High School. His involvement with the theatre led to myriad contacts and friends who shared interests in the arts. Mobley's association with the theatre, on the other hand, provided a reorganization of life in a small town.

Mobley, who began shooting for the theatre in 1962 and continued for twenty-plus years, also shot for the *Moultrie County News*. He had arrived in Sullivan with his family the previous year to work for the Illinois Farm Bureau. Photography was always something he did on the side, but once in Sullivan, his skill put him in a different light.

> [The theatre and the newspaper] placed me in the public eye. And it gave me instant credibility. I came into Sullivan totally unknown, a no-money background. Sullivan is extremely cliquish. There is this small group of moneyed folk, but I was instantly drawn into their circle because of what I could do and because of my contacts. When I ran for the school board, no one at the paper thought I had a chance, but I was the leading vote-getter the first time I ran.

Mobley began shooting for the theatre using an old Kodak Metalist with flash. "When I found out I could use Tri-X film in theater lighting, I had made the switch to Hasselblad," he said. "It was like having your own studio, and I found I could direct lighting and I could direct people. . . . The theatre folk were used to taking direction, so I did, and it was marvelous."

Picture call was the evening after opening night, immediately after the performance while the actors were still in costume. The play was run backward to photograph all the major scenes. Again, Mobley would immediately process and proof the film to get it all to the theatre the next morning. Some shots would be used for theatre publicity. The actors, especially the apprentices, would also order prints to include in their portfolios.

Copies of the photographs Mobley took of the stars also wound up on the walls at Jibby's. Whether Mobley or Jibby Florini originally suggested the practice that helped give the bar the nickname "Sardi's of Sullivan" is unclear. Both men give each other credit. But whoever did come up with the idea, the consequence was mutually beneficial. It gave Mobley a gallery for his work with a mixed audience, and, for Florini, it added to the lure and lore of his place.

After the performance, but before the opening night party officially got under way, a press conference was held with the star, director, producer, and occasionally supporting members of the cast. The press conference was a later addition to the season's activities, begun around 1970. The press conference supplied area newspapers with even more access to the theatre and the stars, but the *Moultrie County News* provided primary coverage of the theatre.

From the beginning, the *News* and the theatre had a close relationship. One of the two local weekly newspapers, the *Moultrie County News* did much to spread the word of the institution that made the community unique. What is ironic is that the family behind the newspaper bought it because of the theatre.

The *News* began covering and commenting in editorials on the theatre from the first season. The paper's owners, the Lippincott family, sold the paper in 1961 to Bob and Marion Best, who faced a decision to buy a newspaper business in either Sullivan or Clinton, Missouri. Marion Best, the publisher since her husband's death in 1993, said there had been nothing about the theatre in either the business prospectus or in any of the information about Sullivan. The Bests still had their doubts about purchasing the newspaper when, Bob noted in his 21 July 1966 column, they heard Jack Haskell being interviewed by Jack Paar and say he was going to Sullivan, Illinois, to do *Brigadoon*. "Well, we figured that any small town that was getting plugs on network television was bound to be doing something other than wither on the vine—and we had seen a lot of withering towns by that time—so here we came."

The *News* began reviewing The Little Theatre's productions in 1963 with the production of *Harvey*. Bob and Marion Best pre-

sumed that because the theatre was featuring recognizable performers in familiar shows, published reviews would serve no purpose.
According to Marion Best, however, Violet Carlson, who appeared
in *Harvey* with Joe E. Brown, said the actors deserved an honest,
published critique of a performance, even though a person may have
been in a particular role for months or years.

Over the years, the Bests and their newspaper became integral
members and ardent supporters of the community, as well as an
indispensable local business. The theatre gave the local paper a
wealth of intriguing stories and features, the likes of which were not
seen in most small-town newspapers. In return, the *News* gave the
theatre consistently professional coverage in a newspaper that had
a circulation much wider than just Moultrie County. The *News* also
did the majority of the printing for the theatre. In 1981, after Little
had left Sullivan and the theatre was dark for a season, Bob and
Marion Best would play a vital role in restarting the theatre.

During the star years, other businesses and people were drawn into
the theatre's routine to varying extents and outcomes. In most cases,
however, the product of such an association was not necessarily
dramatically increased profits but an enduring personal connection.

An example of one business was the hardware store around the
corner from the theatre. According to Richard Isaacs, owner of
Kaskia True Value from 1965 to 1990, his proximity to the theatre
made it very handy for the theatre to use his store for much of their
scenery and set work. "I got to know a lot of the people during the
period of time that they were here year after year and built a good
relationship." Isaacs, too, would be instrumental in keeping the theatre going and championing the theatre's economic contributions
to the area.

Another person drawn into the theatre's realm was Sharon White,
who designed and made costumes starting in 1973. Her husband,
Ron, joined a local pharmacy the preceding year and, according to
White, she was somewhat hesitant about the move. "The only reason that I came, willingly, to Sullivan was because I knew the theatre was here and I could get involved with it and that would save
me and it did."

For White, the theatre made an aspect of life in a small town
extraordinary. She summed up the frustrations and rewards when
she described costuming for Leonard Nimoy in *One Flew over the*

Cuckoo's Nest in 1974. "As McMurphy, [Nimoy] was this rough, tough . . . looking character and he decided it would be more macho if he had a tattoo. I would go in every evening before the show and paint tattoos on his arm. That is sort of an intimate thing. . . . Here I am with Mr. Spock, for god's sakes, and I am painting pictures on his arms. I couldn't have met Mr. Spock if The Little Theatre On The Square didn't exist."

White continued to describe how Nimoy took over as director and noted some of the challenges associated with costuming such a play. "The person that Guy hired turned out to be such a washout that, early in rehearsal, [Nimoy] took over and did direct . . . it was very powerful. [*Cuckoo's Nest*] kind of stretched me as a costumer because the whole thing takes place in an insane asylum and I had to sew things like straitjackets. . . . I was running around the mental health clinic saying, 'Do you have a photograph of a straitjacket? I have to make one.'"

The Whites, like many others, would also play a crucial role in keeping the theatre going. "I have had more fun," said Sharon White. "And the people . . . another reason we keep it going is the people. We have met people and become friends with people that we never would have ever known if it hadn't been for the theatre."

As The Little Theatre On The Square began to make a name for itself and its reputation began to expand throughout the area, its influence permeated substantial parts of daily life in Sullivan. The theatre provided opportunities for many people that otherwise would have unlikely existed in such a community. The theatre also introduced into the community people that were distinct in many ways from most area residents. These people enriched the lives of many, but they also galled a few.

4

SOCIAL CONSEQUENCES OF THE THEATRE IN SULLIVAN

B y the mid-1960s, the theatre had settled into a pattern of successful productions and increasing recognition, including being heralded as "The Miracle of Sullivan" by the *St. Louis Globe Democrat*. The theatre also became familiar fodder for editorials in the local newspaper exclaiming its virtues and gently browbeating readers who had yet to experience the magic of a live production. What the local editorials only alluded to but the larger papers did mention, if only in passing, was that the theatre was not collectively embraced.

Guy S. Little Jr. had purchased the Grand Theatre in 1963 and officially changed the name from Summer of Musicals to The Little Theatre On The Square. In a photograph on the cover of the Sunday magazine of the *Globe Democrat,* he wore red hair and wire-rim glasses, in character for one of his various roles. In addition to all of his other responsibilities, Little cast himself in a couple of productions during most seasons.

The *Globe Democrat* article—as well as local newspaper coverage and a 1968 feature in *Marathon World,* the Marathon Oil company magazine—focused on the novelty of a professional theatre in the middle of a corn town that attracts busloads of people to see well-known actors. Even the title, "The Miracle of Sullivan," suggests divine involvement for such an unlikely scenario to work. No article, however, was so idealistic as to ignore the fact that not everybody in Sullivan was enamored with the theatre, even from the very beginning.

Despite the storybook circumstances surrounding the beginning of the theatre, it was a shock to the senses and sensibilities of a small, homogeneous, church-going community in 1957. The theatre became a catalyst, introducing to Sullivan any number of unknown social and political forces. That is, of course, not to say the people of Sullivan would *never* have been exposed to African Americans, homosexuality, and a big-city liberalism. The theatre and the people it brought into town simply accelerated the rate at which the effects of dealing with such issues were felt.

At one end of the spectrum of influences, the theatre introduced an aspect of the city into a small farming town with one stoplight. At the other end, the theatre distorted one's perspective of what such a small town should be and what one could expect from it. These expectations extended to the uses of familiar space and interactions with different types of people. This consequence is amplified by the fact that American society, in general, was much more sheltered, with considerably less disagreeable subject matter broadcast on only three television networks, all enveloped by 1950s ideals and morality.

As noted by long-time residents, something different about Sullivan allowed for the theatre's success, beyond the fact that the producer was a hometown boy. Many people identified particular characteristics—an affluence, an openness, a homogeneity more akin to unity than exclusivity—that distinguished Sullivan from other small towns. These nuances may very well have helped the theatre survive; however, they did not make Sullivan a liberal rival of Champaign-Urbana. Tavern owner Jibby Florini best summed up the general attitude. "In the early years there was a lot of prejudice about the theatre because Sullivan is a small town, and they don't like change."

Prejudice against the actors even extended to how local businesses interacted with them. Bill Stubblefield, who owned a Sullivan car dealership, remembered when people from the theatre wanted to rent or lease cars, and the insurance company said it did not allow professional actors to drive the cars it insured.

Even though Little had the advantage of being a hometown boy, the ways in which area residents would perceive and respond to his new business were unclear. Joe Florini, Jibby's son, went so far as to call the Sullivan of 1957 "prudish," with the theatre bringing into the community an element of the city at a time when the community was not prepared to accept it. "The theatre brought to a small town a whole different language than what you saw in the movies in that era. They swore, cussed. . . . I think the churches still have a hard time with that but they had a really hard time with it at that point." Similarly, Jean Florini, Joe's wife, mentioned being surprised at the volatile temperaments of some of the actors. In addition, the articles in the *Globe Democrat* and *Marathon World* quote residents who would not go to the theatre or any place where they might hear profanity or that would take the Lord's name in vain.

Many locals expressed a sentiment toward the theatre similar to that toward the local taverns. One might expect such drinking establishments to open their doors for, if not embrace as Jibby's Tavern did, their fellow outcasts. Instead, they turned their backs. "The other places," according to Jibby Florini, "kind of looked down their noses at the actors. I made them welcome." Not only did Florini make the theatre people feel welcome, the theatre helped to make his business more reputable and consuming alcohol more socially acceptable.

Sullivan was never dry, as were other communities in Moultrie County, but it had a very active Women's Christian Temperance Union. Jibby's daughter-in-law, Jean, who came from nearby Bethany, which was dry, was brought up in a family that believed taverns to be sinful places. Jibby's own mother-in-law, an active member of the WCTU, had never set foot into the bar until the theatre came to town. According to Jibby, she eventually worked in the bar's kitchen.

> I had the bar [for] years before [Ruth's] mother ever set foot in here. She thought I was running a whorehouse. Know what changed her? Penny was playing over there . . . Rosemary Prinz. The sweet young thing that all the little old ladies loved. I loved her, too. So I took her [mother-in-law] to see Penny. And I said, "Now Gramma, you want to see Penny and meet her, you have to come in to Jibby's." So she comes in. She looks around. I have Doc Best over there and

I think the mayor is in here. The people of town . . . good people. I introduced her to Penny. She was in heaven. I couldn't keep her out of here after that. Came up every night. She'd call me up sometime and I'd say "I don't need you tonight, I have plenty." "Well, I'll come up and work for nothing."

Similarly, Kate Livergood's mother had also never been in Jibby's until Rosemary Prinz came to town. According to Livergood, her mother described going into the bar to meet the soap opera star, then afterwards sitting down to have coffee at the "counter."

Not only did the theatre change attitudes among teetotalers about a place such as Jibby's, it affected perceptions of who could be seen drinking in a bar. Among those who would not dare to be seen in Jibby's, even if they drank, were schoolteachers. They instead took advantage of Jibby's package liquor business and picked up their bottles or six-packs at the bar's back door.

Margaret Hollowell, the speech pathologist for the school district, remembered returning to Sullivan in the early 1960s after being away for a decade and being surprised at how much had changed. "The first time I went into Jibby's when I first came back to Sullivan . . . the first people I met in there were parents of first-graders I had in therapy. I thought, 'Oh, I am going to lose my job.'" But she did not. Instead, Hollowell said, she and the parents of her students spent the evening talking about the children, much to the parents' delight.

Before the theatre, Jibby's customers were primarily farmers and workers from the Brown Shoe Company, "just ordinary people you'd find in a small town." He also sponsored a number of softball and bowling teams, activities, according to Ray Oldenburg (1997), that substantially enhanced the reputability of taverns and helped integrate them into the community. It was also something of which Florini was very conscious. Active in community organizations, Florini considered himself something of a promoter, but one also concerned with maintaining a respectable reputation. "I used to advertise the spot for fun," but, said Florini, "with good order. That is very important and it really paid off."

When the theatre first opened, Jibby's was classified as a tavern and no one under twenty-one years old was even allowed in the place, much less to be served. The law allowing underage people into a tavern changed in the mid-1960s, but Jibby never ran the risk of serving to minors or serving after the one A.M. curfew.

In a relatively short period, Jibby's became the place to go before the theatre for dinner and, especially, after the performance to mingle with the actors. As Joe Florini recalled, the actors "changed clothes, took their makeup off, came over, and you could talk to them. You could get their autographs, visit, and it was close contact. That was a neat concept, and it was great for business."

Being the self-proclaimed promoter, Jibby took advantage of the after-theatre attraction. He eventually wound up tripling the size of his business. He expanded his menu from sandwiches and pizza, for which he was well known, to other items. "I'd have a table of four, six, or eight come in and ask me where to go eat," said Florini. Instead of turning groups of theatergoers away, he started serving steaks. It was a decision that, according to Florini, "just blew the roof off the business."

Ruth Florini, Jibby's wife, would often help out in the evenings, especially once their children were older. She said they both made it a point to mingle and try to talk to everyone. They got to know who had what season tickets for what nights and looked forward to seeing their favorite people.

Jibby said he would often be offered twenty dollars for a table but always turned it down because it was not fair to the locals. He never forgot that the theatre season ran only during the summer and that he had to cater to his regular customers for the rest of the year. He even kept this in mind when he was considering remodeling.

Jibby recalled a conversation with Pat O'Brien, one of the theatre and tavern regulars, in which the decor of the bar was discussed:

> Pat O'Brien would come back every year and he would look around and say "What are you doing now?" and I would tell him. I said, "You know, I am on the borderline here, Pat. My wife wants to carpet this. She wants to put flowers here and captain's chairs. . . ." The Red Fox had opened and they had all of that. I said, "There will be no damned flowers in this place. This is a tavern." I said, "I can afford to carpet, put in [captains] chairs but if I do . . . you know, you guys are just here three months in the summer. My locals . . . Brown Shoe factory and the farmers . . . come in here every day. And as I said, there is a lot of animosity about that theatre. I said, "They will blackball me if I get too fancy. I ain't gonna do it." He [Pat O'Brien]

looked around and said, "I have been all over the world. Your place is nice enough for everybody but not too nice for anybody."

During the late 1960s, the Red Fox, a restaurant, opened on the east side of the square. Its environs and decor were considerably different from Jibby's, and they tended to attract a different clientele, especially among the nontheatre crowds, though there was much crossover between both groups. Some of Jibby's customers thought the Red Fox would take away some of his business, to which he gave a typical Jibby reply. "You know, I have been here way before they started and I'll be here a hell of a lot longer after they close." And he was certainly correct. The Red Fox had several different owners and opened and closed as many times. The building where the restaurant used to be is now an insurance office. Jibby's Tavern still exists though Jibby Florini has long since retired.

Jibby's Tavern did not simply cater to the theatre crowds during the summer and to locals during the rest of the year. Locals and theatre people were often at the bar at the same time. Occasionally, the encounters, as with Pat O'Brien or Ann B. Davis, were enjoyable for everyone. Other times, however, less-than-friendly words were said. Such exchanges between locals and theatre people did not define the character of the theatre season but did occur often enough to augment the vocabulary of the area.

SHOWDOGS AND TOWNIES

Contact between the stars and Sullivan residents was rarely confrontational. The stars tended to be easily recognizable or well known, and the surprise to Sullivan residents was how normal they seemed. As the 1968 article for *Marathon World* mentioned, "While the Sullivanians are mostly nonchalant about show people, the stars themselves become zealots about Sullivan." If central Illinois did not qualify as a land of luxury or leisure, it certainly qualified as a land of quiet and relaxation away from places like New York, Los Angeles, or Chicago, and many returned for that reason. One in particular found central Illinois to be more homelike than most.

Peter Palmer first appeared in Sullivan in 1962 and, over the years, returned thirteen times. Originally from St. Louis, Palmer played football for the University of Illinois. He also sang the national anthem before the games dressed in his football uniform.

Palmer had appeared opposite Jerili Little in *Roberta* while they were both students at the U. of I. Palmer originated the role of *Li'l Abner* on Broadway in 1956 and recreated the role at The Little Theatre in 1972. Sullivan became so much of a second home to him, he chose to announce his engagement to Aniko Farrell there in 1966. Beginning in 1968, the two of them performed together in Sullivan half a dozen times.

In general, there was conviviality between the stars and local residents that the latter remembered warmly, adding to the collection of positive memories of the theatre in town. Bill Stubblefield, a local businessman who pitched in to build sets the first year but never became a great theatre buff, recalled Pat O'Brien's version of fun down at Jibby's.

> [Pat O'Brien would] get on an old pair of bib overalls and sit down with the clientele and get to spinning yarns with them and he was quite a baseball nut. He could quote the stat book and he would bet with these guys. . . . They knew who he was and didn't care. He'd buy them a beer and he was one of them. He would make several bets about baseball records or pitcher's records or whatever, and he would always be right. So when he would get done he would leave the money on the counter for them to drink up after he left.

Given the right audience, according to Jibby Florini, O'Brien would also occasionally reenact the "win-one-for-the-Gipper" scene from *The Knute Rockne Story*, all for a schooner of beer.

Another less typical but equally memorable evening at Jibby's occurred with Ann B. Davis in 1963. She was still playing Schultzy on *The Bob Cummings Show* when she appeared at The Little Theatre in *Everybody Loves Opal*. One night, said Florini, while at Jibby's after the show, she dashed off to Mamie Palmer's house to get her guitar for a sing-along in which many people participated.

> The actors and the local people, too, mixing together. Don't forget, there was animosity. . . . They all got in there and were singing with them. We sang until one thirty and I wanted to go beyond that. We weren't serving drinks. But at that time, we had a tough policeman. He'd shine the spotlight in, and we had to get them out. We were having so much fun, you don't want it to end. I suppose he thought I was selling drinks, but I wasn't. I wouldn't dare sell one, not with him out there.

While encounters with the top-billed actors may have been fun and memorable, the star was only one person out of scores of people who were part of every theatre season. It was this group of people—Equity actors in supporting roles, the apprentices, and technical staff—who were the most visible and who had the most contact with local residents. It was also this group, especially the apprentices, who got dubbed "showdogs" beginning in the early 1960s.

The origins of the term "showdog" are questionable. According to Seth Reines, veteran of many seasons of summer stock and The Little Theatre's current artistic director, "showdog" is not a familiar term within the theatre scene and would seem to be unique to Sullivan. The term was used by locals to refer to theatre people, in part because they were so distinct from the rest of the community. The original recipients of such a nickname were probably overtly gay or flamboyant male apprentices.

An older actor suggested the word "showdog" originated in vaudeville and referred to second-tier acts or those that came immediately before or after the headliner, the spot often reserved for canine acts. Sullivan residents could have become familiar with the word in conversation with a star such as Joe E. Brown, a former vaudevillian himself who was known to enjoy socializing with locals in places like a barbershop.

This theory is supported by David Mobley, the theatre's photographer, who recalled stories of "showdog" originating in Ralph's barbershop and being used to refer to two male apprentices caught in a compromising position on the courthouse lawn. Others do not attribute the origins of "showdog" to the barbershop but do associate it with a recollection of homosexual activity on the square.

The connotation of the term changed through the 1960s and early 1970s and came to mean any person associated with the theatre, regardless of sexual orientation. The usual recipients of the insult, however, were still the apprentices. The current familiar community memory of an encounter with a "showdog" is of high school students—usually boys—cruising the square, a primary social activity. The boys would yell "showdog" and bark at the theatre apprentices in front of the theatre or on the courthouse lawn across from the theatre. The apprentices, in turn, would yell "townie" back to the kids in the car.

Such exchanges obviously occurred in places other than the courthouse lawn, but that seems to be the location fixed in people's memories. As previously mentioned, the theatre had limited backstage, wing, and rehearsal spaces. The rehearsal studio was an empty, unair-conditioned retail space around the corner from the theatre on Washington Street and, in a central Illinois summer, could become intolerably hot. As a result, activities spilled outside. Often, however, apprentices simply took breaks or sat on the courthouse lawn to rest. This all became part of the community's memory, forever documented by a reference in the 31 July 1974 *Los Angeles Times* feature entitled "Profile of a Small, Midwestern Town" by Bella Stumbo.

On the whole, the article was patronizing, painting Sullivan residents as dimwitted or eccentric, and the theatre as a quaint enterprise. While, on one hand, the theatre created an economic windfall for local merchants, a less desirable byproduct is, according to Stumbo quoting local theatre foes, "that fairies are lollygagging on the courthouse lawn all year long."

Sharon White remembered an exchange from the early 1970s, a discussion of the flamboyant behavior of the theatre people and something about lollygagging on the courthouse lawn, a probable reference to the Stumbo article. White's memory included Guy S. Little Sr., the theatre owner's father—whose office was right across the street from the courthouse—saying, "If they're going to be doing it out there on the courthouse lawn, I'm gonna take down these drapes so I can watch."

Whether Guy Sr. actually expressed an interest in the activities going on outside his window is not really relevant. What is true is, regardless of distraction—dancers practicing, gays lollygagging, or apprentices yelling retorts to high school students—the courthouse lawn became as much of a stage as did the official performance space inside the theatre. The impromptu public stage also turned bystanders into active audience members with no ticket necessary to witness any range of spectacle.

The courthouse square was used as a stage on a very regular basis for community activities. Any type of parade, but especially the homecoming parade, always went around the square with people sitting or standing on both sides of the streets to watch. Santa Claus was also greeted with a small parade the Saturday morning after Thanksgiving, and he held court in a little red house parked on the west side of the courthouse lawn. These were all sanctioned and welcomed activities for such a place; however, using the Lincoln Eighth Judicial Circuit Marker as a ballet barre apparently was not.

Exchanges between "showdogs" and "townies" occurred in bars as well, including Jibby's, though Jibby Florini kept such activity to a minimum. David Mobley recalled hearing stories of incidents that occurred shortly after the theatre opened and could have become ugly. He never saw any himself. "I saw some drunks insult some other drunks, but nobody gave a shit. And, again, if a townie was outnumbered, he generally kept his mouth shut and vice versa."

Jack Milo, an actor who has been a regular part of the theatre since 1981, experienced being called a "showdog" during his first few years in Sullivan. "I just happened to be in a pub one night and some guy was just mouthing off about the theatre and calling them 'showdogs.' I got right into his face and I said, 'I'm a "showdog." You got problem with that?' And I didn't have to worry about it anymore . . . and I have not heard the expression for a while."

The term still is used, but it has been co-opted by members of the theatre company and is used in a jocular manner among themselves. Michael Haws, an actor who grew up in Moultrie County, never called anyone a "showdog" but remembered being in a car with high school friends who did. Circumstances had changed dramatically by the time Haws returned to Sullivan as an Equity actor in the late 1980s. He had not heard the word from anyone in the community for a long time, but it did pop up in an unlikely place. "Jibby's restaurant has a meal for us in between our final dress rehearsal and preview on Tuesdays. Last year, one of the waitresses let it slip that this meal was referred to as 'showdog night.'" Haws has also acquired "showdog" as a nickname among some of the other members of the company.

Part of what made a theatre person a "showdog" was that it originally was easy to distinguish one associated with the theatre from community residents by dress, hairstyle, carriage, et cetera. Over time, the distinctions became less apparent. On one hand, community members began to better relate to the theatre. On the other, however, styles changed, as Sharon White pointed out. "Let's face it, ordinary kids today are as weird as the 'showdogs' were in those days. They all dress funny; they all wear weird hairdos. Apprentices wear earrings; local kids wear earrings. It would have been a big deal in 1981. In 1996, you don't even notice it."

The Theatre and Racial Diversity

Moultrie County has never been a bastion of racial or cultural diversity. In the early sixties, around the same time Sullivan residents were labeling "showdogs," there were only fourteen nonwhites noted in the census among a county population of almost fourteen thousand. Even now, according to the 1990 census, the nonwhite population of Moultrie County is forty-eight people. But, as with encounters between "showdogs" and "townies," the issue of race never escalated beyond verbal exchanges. In fact, the perceptions of African Americans among Sullivan residents showed changes over time similar to those of the "showdogs."

The first African American actor Guy Little hired was an Equity actor from New York, Michael Wright, who, ironically, was from Shelbyville, a somewhat larger town twenty miles southeast of Sullivan. Wright was cast in *Bloomer Girl,* a musical described in the 3 August 1961 *Moultrie County News* as "a salute to the Civil War centennial . . . a modern musical comedy with old world charm about Dolly Bloomer."

Collective memories of people in Sullivan in 1961 recalled either a sunset law on the books or an unspoken rule that no black man would be caught in Sullivan after the sun went down, much less spend the night. Wright, as an Equity actor, stayed with a local couple as most other performers did. Rumor also had select area residents threatening to blow up the theatre or close it down for good. Not only did nothing like this happen, it never rose above gossip.

Nowhere in the coverage of the 1961 season in the *Moultrie County News* is it mentioned that Michael Wright was African American or that there were any African American apprentices. It is also not an issue touched on in editorials or letters to the editor. The matter of race has been relegated to anecdotes and memory.

Jibby Florini witnessed local sentiment about having African Americans in town on a couple of occasions at his bar. But just as he kept all confrontations between locals and theatre people down, he also kept confrontations about race in check. "[Wright] came in here, and I had to stop a couple guys from going over and challenging him. . . . They wanted him thrown out and so on."

Another time, Bob Gwaltney, an actor and regular with the theatre since the first season, was sitting at the other side of the bar. He was apparently a regular at Jibby's as well. According to Florini, "I am mixing drinks in front of [Gwaltney]. He is telling Michael how, if he doesn't get a laugh where he is supposed to, he is brokenhearted. Michael said, 'You know, Bob, I have been listening to you for two months with all your troubles. I am the only black man in this white man's town.' I really got a kick out of that so I set him up a drink. Now that is trouble."

It should be noted that during the years The Little Theatre operated as a star theatre, the only African American stars were Butterfly McQueen in 1967 in *Showboat,* though not in a starring role, and Isabel Sanford in 1977 in *And Mama Makes Three.* Since the demise of the star system, the theatre has continued to hire African American Equity actors, apprentices, and techies. In recent years, there has been a somewhat ironic twist to the presence of African Americans in town. There seems to be a distinct level of acceptance, but only as long as they are with the theatre.

The Little Theatre had hired an African American designer shortly after Seth Reines, the current artistic director, took over in 1988. According to Reines, the designer would say, "'How do they know I am from this theatre?' I said, 'Well, look around.' I don't know why there aren't blacks in this community. He decided there was some conspiracy going on. I said, 'No, I don't think so.'" While Reines noted the distinct lack of racial tension he experienced in Cumberland County, Tennessee, he said he still had a hard time attracting African American performers to the company, creating the kind of diverse cast he wanted.

Chuck Bell, a semiregular since 1988, described a similar situation, which occurred during the 1995 season.

Last year we had a black singer from Indianapolis, she was maybe twenty-three, twenty-four. . . . She went into a bar [Cousins] across the street one night. The bartender gave her a real hard time and suggested that maybe that wasn't the place for her to drink. I went in the next night and got to talking with the bartender. I had never been in there before. She said, "You work for the theatre, right?" I said, "Yeah." "Do you have a black woman working over there?" I said, "Yeah. Why?" "Oh, well, you tell her she is welcome in here anytime. I didn't know she worked for the theatre. She came in last night, and I didn't know what to do with her. We don't usually see black people in here."

HAIR IN THE HEARTLAND

Relations between the community and the theatre peaked in 1974 with the production of *Hair*. On one hand, the production was a flash in the pan, a blip on the screen of forty years worth of memorable but uneventful theatre. The reason this one production received such attention, according to Sharon White, who worked on costumes for *Hair*, was because it was something different. "It was shocking, and ninety-nine and forty-four hundredths of what went on in that theatre and still goes on in that theatre is not shocking."

On the other hand, however, the protests and concerns voiced during the production of *Hair* revealed a rift in the community. Although spurred by the theatre's choice of production, the conflict exposed pockets of tightly held beliefs largely unrelated to the theatre but rather perceptions of and reactions to larger social issues. While *Hair* gave residents of a small town something juicy to talk about, only a small minority of people was resolutely opposed.

Hair is antithetical to the type and style of show, musical or drama, produced at The Little Theatre. From 1957 to 1997, the most frequently produced show was *Oklahoma!*, followed closely by *Fiddler on the Roof* and *Guys and Dolls*. Productions during Guy Little's tenure that were notably uncharacteristic were *Who's Afraid of Virginia Woolf?* with Mercedes McCambridge in 1967, Stephen Sondheim's *Company* with Janis Paige in 1972, and *Equus* with John Gavin in 1977. Even after Little's departure in 1979, the kind of show produced varied only marginally from the tradition that had been set. Out of forty-plus years of theatre in Sullivan, *Hair* was by far the aberration; it also tended to be something of a departure from the traditional American musical.

Hair opened off-Broadway in 1967, originally produced by Joseph Papp, producer of the New York Shakespeare Theatre. The script was first brought to Papp's attention by authors and lyricists Gerome Ragni and James Rado while on a train. After an initial aversion, Papp, in an 11 April 1988 *New York* magazine article, described being taken by a scene in particular, "a scene about young people and loneliness and parents." Papp said people thought he was crazy for producing *Hair,* and he did not anticipate a success. "[*Hair*] has a kind of documentary character. I wasn't thinking in large terms of success then. . . . I wanted to do things that were important. I never wanted to take the show to Broadway, I thought it was too pure to go to Broadway."

After *Hair*'s eight-week run at New York's Public Theatre, it played briefly at Cheetah, a New York discotheque, before opening on Broadway in April 1968. The Broadway production, which ran for 1,742 performances, was directed by Tom O'Horgan and produced by Michael Butler, an Illinois Democratic party supporter, heir to a Chicago-area family fortune, and theatre novice. Under O'Horgan and Butler, *Hair* took on the qualities for which it would become nationally known. O'Horgan revised and restaged the production, including adding the nude scene at the end of the first act.

In a 1967 *Newsweek* review of the Papp production, Jack Kroll described *Hair* as a kind of "free-form, plotless 'Oh, What a Happy Hippiedom,'" but one that "ignites the key issues of the lost-and-found generation—youth vs. age, sex, love, the draft, race, drugs, Vietnam—into a vivid uproar. . . ." In a 1968 *Newsweek* review of the Broadway production, Kroll said there was a kinetic drive in the "new *Hair*." His only criticism of the nude scene was that it was not lit well enough to "really see this fleshy manifesto of the beautiful young people who give their all. . . ." He ended by saying there was something hard, grabby, and slightly corrupt about O'Horgan's virtuosity, "like Busby Berkeley gone bitchy."

Joseph Papp was not pleased with the Broadway production. According to *New York* magazine, he thought it had lost some of its innocence with a cast of actors who were interested in making money rather than hippies who wanted to make a statement. However, as John Joy discussed in his 1975 dissertation, the O'Horgan production brought to a much wider audience a message of defiance and dissatisfaction that had accumulated over an entire decade and affected an entire generation. "Never mind that it was vulgar, loud, sloppy, unclear, unstructured" (133).

In 1968, *Hair* was a major departure from the traditional Broadway musical form. It was, according to Barbara Horn (1982), the first nonbook musical based more on the music, with a strong social and political ideology instead of a plot. Described by critics as "an event," "a spectacle," even as "a tourist attraction," *Hair* established a theatrical precedent for later works such as *A Chorus Line* and *Cats*.

Despite what contribution *Hair* may have made to American musical theatre, it garnered attention because of its liberal politics and the nude scene. And, as road companies, or Tribes, opened around the country, *Hair* inspired mixed reviews and more than its share of protests. In Washington, D.C., according to Horn (1982), groups ranging from the Smite Smut League to the Gay Liberation League picketed the front of the theatre. In St. Paul, local clergy released white mice in the theatre hoping to scare audience members. And, in Boston, an attempt to prohibit public obscenities forced producer Michael Butler to close an indefinite run for six weeks rather than compromise the show's integrity. In *P.B.I.C., Inc. v. Garret H. Byrne* (313 F.Supp 757 D.Mass. [1970]), the U.S. District Court held that neither Massachusetts statute proscribing open and gross lewdness nor common-law crime of indecent exposure could be applied to live theatrical productions. It was a law, noted Circuit Judge Coffin, that prevented audiences from deciding the merits of the show for themselves and made the cast members face possible imprisonment on sex charges or loss of livelihood if the show closed.

The Midwest also had its share of *Hair* cases as well. Noting the twentieth anniversary of *Hair* in the 20 January 1991 *St. Louis Post-Dispatch,* theatre critic Joe Pollack recalled local reaction to the 1971 production. Because of the national attention *Hair* received, a member of the board of aldermen proposed a bill that would have prohibited the nude scene more than a year before the play was to open. A substitute bill that banned obscenities but did not mention nudity was passed. The show's producers, in turn, sought a temporary restraining order to prevent enforcement of the ordinance. A St. Louis judge saw the Kansas City production—a production that had its fill of protests—and, according to Pollack, praised its theatrical qualities, but also called it "a vulgar, filthy play still entitled to the protection of the first amendment."

Whatever the consequence of the protests, John Joy (1975) asserts that the negative attention actually increased public support (i.e., ticket sales), if only to see what the fuss was about. This is not unlike what occurred with the production in Sullivan.

Guy Little announced in December 1973 that there would be no holiday production due to the energy crisis and a lack of available stars but scheduled a two-week run of *Hair* as a special non-subscription production to open in March. The regular season was set to begin the following month. At that point, nobody seemed to take notice. Over the course of the next two months, however, some people had apparently taken a second look.

The First Church of God in Sullivan took out a full-page ad in the 21 February 1974 *Moultrie County News*. It said, "We, the undersigned citizens of Sullivan and surrounding area, are *STRONGLY* opposed to the presentation of the Broadway play *Hair* at The Little Theatre On The Square. This play has nudity, profanity, obscenity, suggestive songs, and praises the use of drugs. We are not in favor of this type of play *EVER* being presented in the Sullivan area."

Fifty-five members of the congregation, led by the Reverend James Fox, had signed the ad. According to local memory, a couple of the people whose names appeared on the protest said they thought the ad would just include the name of the church, not list the fifty-five names individually. Many of the names were easily recognizable as long-time Sullivan residents; very few, if any, were noted to be theatre patrons or supporters.

The protest against *Hair* attracted much attention. Locally, the Church of God protest started a fervent campaign of letters to the editor of the *Moultrie County News,* letters that had little to do with the theatre but more to do with Christian behavior and freedom of expression. A letter appeared in the 28 February *News* offering an alternative point of view.

> As for the things that may be presented in the musical, i.e. nudity, profanity, etc., I think the signers may be losing sight of reality a little. Do you really think that Mr. Little will do anything to put Sullivan in total uproar? . . . We live in a more liberal society today than in past generations. Whether the signers agree with the concepts of today or "STRONGLY oppose" them is arbitrary. The point is, there is a difference.

The letters that followed were quite varied. In the 7 March 1974

Moultrie County News, a minister of another Sullivan Protestant church supported *Hair* and essentially called the play Christian because of its antiwar, antikilling, and prolife themes. What distressed him was the anti-Christian behavior between members of the same community. People may and will disagree, he wrote, but it can be done in "a way that is loving and Christian and express real concern over issues and not over personalities."

A letter in the same issue maintained that the number of people who signed the original ad would have swelled from fifty-five to one thousand had the Reverend Fox had more time to collect signatures. The letter writer considered *Hair* to be inherently anti-Christian, being supported by hypocrites and heretics, including churches that were blind to the "true gospel." "The production of *Hair* is nothing more than a play glorifying immorality. If you are in doubt of this, just check it out, just check any of the ratings listed in magazines and see how it is rated."

The story of *Hair* in Sullivan was being covered by area newspapers and television, and had been picked up by United Press International before opening night. In a 16 March 1974 article in the *Charleston (Ill.) Times-Courier,* Guy Little defended *Hair* as a very positive, religious, prolove, antiwar musical. "There are no words that can't be found in the Sullivan Public Library. And it is a nursery rhyme compared to *Oh, Calcutta,* which showed here last summer at the drive-in theatre. No one protested that."

In a wire service article from the *Los Angeles Daily Breeze,* the Reverend James Fox, who organized the protest, said that he and three other ministers along with a group of concerned citizens had "banded together in two weeks of prayer, asking God to intervene and prevent the production." Their prayers were answered, though not in the manner intended: The run of *Hair* was extended by a week.

Hair opened on 16 March to a full house. Theatergoers, waiting for the curtain to rise, were greeted with flowers, handed to them by cast members. The nude scene, which caused so much agitation, occurred at the end of act one. The scene, described by John Joy (1975) as selling more tickets than any striptease, was always optional but came to be expected. It lasted roughly thirty seconds and was done, as noted by critics, in disappointingly low light—except in Sullivan.

Instead of subdued light that created a mood, the scene was, according to Bob Best in his 21 March 1974 *Moultrie County News* review, "about as sexually stimulating as a walk through Allerton Park." The lights were actually brought up. The errant technician was reproached by Little and, for the remainder of the run, the nude scene stayed dimly lit, as originally scripted.

During the weeks of ardent letters to the editor, Bob Best's editorials and columns remained conspicuously free of retort. He did respond to the critics and protesters in his review. He very frankly stated that he did not like *Hair*. "It's not my kind of music, and I hated the period and the mood of the country it represents. I do not like to be reminded of them." He instead suggested it might be time for a musical about pompous legislators making nutty speeches, about greedy energy czars, and "about burglars going free and burglars getting caught," even though he doubted he would like that show six years later. "Whether or not one person likes or dislikes a show is rather immaterial. The important thing is that we have an open society in which millions of persons can pay their money and make their own decisions without fear of social approbation or civil penalty. . . ."

The protest in Sullivan had accomplished the same thing as similar actions around the country—increased ticket sales. The show was originally scheduled to run for two weeks but was extended a week, the first time in the theatre's history a show was extended because of demand for tickets. The review in the 22 March 1974 *Decatur Review* even noted that many people who saw the show during the first two weeks returned to see it again. Little then sent the production to Philadelphia where it played for two weeks at the Locust Street Theatre.

Hair closed in Sullivan on 7 April and the protest cooled quickly, but not before another area church put in another full-page ad inviting members of the cast to come and repent. In the 4 April 1974 *Moultrie County News,* the Reverend G. Sumpter addressed the first half of his protest in the form of a letter to publisher Bob Best questioning his willingness to promote the sentiments of Christians and their cultural contributions as he did for supporters of *Hair*. "It puzzles me," continued Sumpter, "that you have chosen to neglect the feelings (or rather to provoke) of so many home-towners who want to promote Sullivan and its beauty state-wide. 'I calls it a foul ball' against the home-town game of good taste!"

Sumpter continued the us-them dichotomy noting that "we know about the sophistication also of the Jet-set with its ideas of relative-values based on situational ethics. Such philosophy and direction proves to be the broadway to destruction." He offered Acts 3:19–21 as an answer to *Hair* and the people who are "turned on by such so-called liberation and release."

The second half was an invitation to the Tribe, the cast of *Hair*, to visit the church's worship hour and, if possible, repent.

> Although we object to your production now showing in Sullivan, you will find us genuinely interested in you as an individual. . . . Again, if you the "Cast and Tribe" judge we Christians and our stand against your show to be peculiar, we accept the verdict unashamedly. . . . The Church of Christ (Highway Congregation) is respected for its ability to teach Scriptural truth. Should you decide to become one of the Master's disciples, we will provide you with food, friendship, and shelter until you may go your way rejoicing in the Lord!

Included in the invitation to the cast was the suggestion that they had not "done the town in" until they had discovered Sullivan's primary cultural contribution, the area's Christian heritage. At the same time, the sponsors of the page solicited interest in creating a theatre guild, to which they gave the working title, Blue Star Family Theatre, named for the scenic route near Lake Shelbyville.

Occurring in Sullivan at the same time as *Hair*, though receiving only peripheral attention, was streaking. The phenomenon exploded in 1974 all over the country, especially on college campuses, and several stories about *Hair* referred to the craze, though not specifically in Sullivan. Bob Best mentioned streaking in Sullivan in his review of *Hair*, as well as in his column the preceding week. "Streaking, as this year's fad is called, made its appearance in Sullivan when three young men ran across the courthouse lawn at the stroke of midnight [9 March]. We have had various reports on identity but not having been there, we just don't believe all the second-hand reports."

The streakers may very well have been local fellows, but they may also have been actors in town for the production of *Hair*. In other words, they may have been "showdogs." That word, certainly part of the local vernacular, was noticeably absent from letters to the editor and other printed matters relating to the dissension. Whether it was regularly vocalized around the Spot or Jibby's is another matter.

Although the actual uproar over *Hair* lasted barely two months, the memory of the production and subsequent events has remained alive. In addition to a story that is often retold, the primary legacy is the belief that the area churches pose the largest potential collective threat to the theatre's productions. This is supported by the suggestion that Little produced *Godspell* and *Jesus Christ Superstar* during the following season for the shows' Christian appeal. Even twenty years after the fact, the theatre and some of its supporters seek out area church leaders to familiarize them with new productions and to invite groups from their congregations to attend the theatre. This is undeniably wise marketing, but it also is meant to preclude a repeat of "the *Hair* incident" and similar protests based on little more than a show's reputation.

5

THE THEATRE COMES OF AGE

⟨decorative ornament⟩

Between the late 1970s and the late 1980s, circumstances changed dramatically for The Little Theatre On The Square. The theatre and the community had survived the 1974 production of *Hair*, but the theatre could not contend with the rising cost of featuring star performers. It was lucky it survived at all. Over the course of the decade, it weathered a half dozen different producers, a number of financial crises, and its only dark season. And while the theatre may not have emerged in the 1990s as the Goodspeed of the Midwest, it found a new stability and, especially, a community and regional appeal that had been lacking.

Hair passed into Sullivan's collective memory, and the rest of the 1974 season occurred with little fanfare. Inflation, plus the rising cost of doing star theatre, forced Guy S. Little Jr. to cut the number of productions the following season from eleven to seven. In general, the type of show he produced did not change. In 1975, he produced both *Godspell* and *Jesus Christ Superstar*, which by all published and anecdotal accounts he specifically marketed to church groups.

Little continued to produce in Sullivan through the 1978 season, but the effort had taken its toll on him. He announced in January 1979 that there would be no twenty-third season. In the 15 January 1979 *Moultrie County News*, Little said the theatre continued to have "wonderful and supportive audiences" for twenty-one seasons but the costs of operation and salaries for stars and supporting actors had become impossible to bear. He went on to say that he felt certain area reviewers and critics had taken the theatre for granted and did nothing to stimulate interest in the theatre among their readers. Later that spring, Little leased the Little Theatre to a new group, and he became the producer–managing director at the Melody Top Theatre in Milwaukee, Wisconsin, where he remained until 1985.

Little's decisions to leave Sullivan and lease the theatre to other people may be considered the end of an era; success without Little would only be a consequence of his legacy and nothing more. Conversely, it may also be looked at, especially when the economic and cultural changes of the 1980s are kept in mind, as, ultimately, the opportunity that kept the theatre going and prevented it from fading to oblivion with mediocre productions starring third-rate aging actors.

Both scenarios are, to some extent, accurate. The Little Theatre had for some time rested on its laurels. This, consequently, affected the audience, as Chuck Bell, a semiregular member of the company since 1988, observed. "I really think the audiences here are different because of the history of the place. It's been around for forty years and this was one of the few places where the stars would come and do their stuff." Bell went on to say that star theatre in its heyday was a lot of fun, but, by the mid 1970s, it had become less about art and more about box office receipts and featuring big names. Emphasis now is on quality repertory with focus on the whole production and not just one "star."

The distinction Bell noted about the audience—the sense of history about the theatre—became a driving force to keep it going, even in a somewhat retailored fashion. "Things have changed," said Sharon White, "and I don't think that is bad. I would venture to say that Guy thinks it's bad because Guy tends to cling to the past and talk about the glory days when he was producing, when he was doing star theatre, when things were done his way. I admit that was terrific but that doesn't play anymore."

White noted that there was still a hunger in central Illinois for professional theatre. This was an appetite The Little Theatre continued to satisfy. In a 30 July 1996 *Champaign News Gazette* review of *A Funny Thing Happened on the Way to the Forum,* the critic wrote, "The Little Theatre is doing yet another outstanding show that is jam-packed with fun. The quality and professionalism of this production and theatre mirrors that of theatres in much larger cities. It is a remarkable group, doing a remarkable job."

The road, however, from 1978 to acclaim by an area critic for "a remarkable group doing a remarkable job" was neither quick nor painless. The theatre went from being a profit-making and independently owned business, buttressed by family support, to a nonprofit enterprise governed by a board of trustees drawn from throughout central Illinois. During this transformation, the theatre stopped featuring star performers and, although remaining an Equity theatre, changed the kind of contract it had with the union. The board also hired a managing director who paid as much attention to the theatre's bottom line as he did to the quality of production. For most of this time, the number of seasonal productions remained at five, primarily musicals, with assorted off-season productions.

The most notable change that occurred after Guy Little left was the theatre's relationship with the surrounding community. After the dark season in 1980, the theatre was rescued by a group of area business and civic leaders determined to keep a unique institution going. The theatre, said Sharon White, one of the original rescuers, "is something not many other little towns can boast of, and I didn't want to see that dry up. I want Sullivan to be the town where The Little Theatre *is,* not where The Little Theatre *was.* And that is what would have happened if the Friends hadn't gotten organized and started producing."

A consequence of the Friends of The Little Theatre taking over, and one continued by Leonard Anderson, hired as general manager in 1987, was a feeling that The Little Theatre became the community's theatre. That is not to say it became a community theatre per se: The Little Theatre remained a professional theatre and a member of Equity. There was, however, an increased sense of ownership that grew, in part, out of contributing money or time. People also realized that they could not take the theatre's existence in Sullivan for granted; it had been dark for one season and there was no reason why it would not permanently close its doors.

Simply because a larger group in Sullivan came to embrace the theatre is not to say that everyone held it dear. The collection of memories that had evolved through the 1960s and 1970s, capped off by the legacies of *Hair* and the "showdog" image, had fermented and grown into piqued, exaggerated tales. As the Friends went about their business, soliciting donations and whatever else to keep the theatre running, they were confronted with these recollections, held up like a sword of righteousness against the evils and ill repute perpetuated by the theatre. The demons of contorted memories have, over the years, been tamed and have themselves become part of the cycle of stories, but not without a concerted effort by the current theatre administration to directly counter misguided expectations.

Sunset over The Little Theatre

Sullivan did not remain without a promise of a theatre season for long. As announced in a press conference in Champaign, Guy Little leased the theatre in March 1979 for the season to Sullivan Theatre, Inc., a nonprofit organization created specifically to run the theatre during that season. The managing directors were Gerald and Barbara Sullivan. Both were connected with the theatre department at Eastern Illinois University in Charleston, but they were not acting under the auspices of the university. The producer was James Grumley, a businessman from the Chicago area, a former official with the national Republican party, and brother to Barbara Sullivan.

The season, which opened 6 June 1979, was announced in the 10 May *Moultrie County News* with "four shows never done in Sullivan before." They were *California Suite, Pippin, A Little Night Music,* and *Little Mary Sunshine. Wait until Dark,* which had previously been done in 1973, was added as a fifth show with a touring company. Only one featured actor that season had previously appeared in Sullivan.

Artistically, the season was best summed up by Marla Jones, an interning theatre critic from the *Decatur Herald and Review.* In her 21 June review of *Pippin,* she pondered whether The Little Theatre should be judged as amateur or professional, or as an uneven mix impossible to grade. In her 22 August review, she compared *Wait until Dark* with the first four productions and concluded the touring cast, with obvious professionalism, fared better than the one-dimensionality of the largely television actors of the season's earlier shows.

Financially, however, the season can be summed up with less ambivalence. Sullivan Theatre, Inc., according to Margaret Hollowell, "lost their shirts." Hollowell, voicing the sentiments of others, concluded that the Sullivans' failure had to do with their choices in programming and casting. They did shows and brought in stars nobody really wanted to see. This included hiring a star Guy Little previously had had the opportunity to engage but had turned down.

The Sullivans also turned away many of the theatre's standard audience members. Sharon White recalled working in the theatre office one day when Guy Little Sr. walked in with a letter that had wound up in his business mail rather than that of the theatre's. The letter was from "something like Aunt Mary's Home for Blue Hair Ladies," White recalled:

> Guy Sr. said, "These are good customers of the theatre. They bring a busload of ladies down here for nearly every production and you are going to want to take good care of them." He gave this letter to Barbara Sullivan. . . . I saw [her] take that letter and throw it in the wastebasket and say "This isn't the kind of audience we want to attract." My reaction was "What do you mean this isn't the kind of audience we want to attract? They are people with green money in their hands. What else do they need?" I couldn't figure out where she was coming from. Somehow, when they came here and produced theatre, [they thought] they were going to have an audience of super people . . . but she threw away a huge group sale. That is when I backed off from the Sullivans.

At the March 1979 press conference, Sullivan Theatre, Inc., announced it had committed $50,000 and would raise $100,000 from the audience. The organization instituted a fund-raising campaign that they called "Angels of The Little Theatre" and featured an ardent plea for money on the second page of each production's program. Their season goal became raising $120,000, the amount needed for the season beyond ticket sales. As part of their appeal, the playbill firmly stated, "No one should think the reopening of The Little Theatre anything but a temporary reprieve. In order to keep The Little Theatre from becoming just a pleasant memory of the way things used to be, it's going to take something more."

The Sullivan Theatre's effort turned out to be only a temporary reprieve; the following season, the theatre was dark. They had scheduled a 1980 season and sold subscription tickets, but that spring, they decided against opening. Grant money they had relied on failed to materialize. Consequently, for many people in the community, Sullivan was very quiet.

Marilyn Stubblefield compared the dark year to when the theatre would close at the end of a season. "More things go on just because the theatre is here and you miss it at the end of the season. Everything stops and that's just the way it was when the theatre was down."

In a similar way, Sharon White described an emptiness. "When a theatre is not open, they say it's 'dark' and it was really, really dark. A light went out in the community and I just don't mean the lights in the marquee. I am sure you would find people in this town who would disagree and say that whether or not that theatre lives or dies couldn't mean less." She continued to say this is because these people have never been inside the theatre and have no idea what goes on.

White's statement about Sullivan residents not caring one way or another about the theatre's survival touches on an argument that would become, and today continues to be, central to the theatre's existence. When Guy Little ran the theatre, it was a profit-making business supported by family efforts. Its economic impact on the city of Sullivan was largely described in anecdotal terms, as in the effects the theatre had on Jibby's Tavern or the Red Fox restaurant. Even after Little left and the theatre became a nonprofit organization—especially after the Friends of The Little Theatre took over— there seemed to be the expectation that the theatre was still "just another business" and had to justify its existence economically.

Richard Isaacs, former owner of Kaskia True Value Hardware and an original Friend, summed up the observations of many regarding the economic impact theatergoers had on Sullivan businesses. In general, Isaacs found most people who came to the theatre would usually only attend the performance and leave, or have dinner before or after the show, then leave. Audience members might window shop but would rarely make anything more than minimal purchases from merchants around the square. Aside from the theatre box office, local service stations, restaurants, and bars took in the bulk of theatergoers' dollars.

Isaacs went on to point out something that those less enamored with the theatre seem hesitant to point out: the aggregate effect of theatre-associated spending in town.

> We have the theatre itself spending money in the local economy and we have people coming to the theatre spending money in the local economy and, together, [they] represent a major amount of new money. . . . A lot of people do not recognize that because they do not get a direct benefit. In their mind, [because] no one from the theatre, whether it is an employee or a patron, comes to their place of business, they view it as they don't get it. They forget that [the theatre] used to spend that money with me and then I would have extra money to go spend it with somebody else or my employees would. . . . I feel strongly that everyone got a major benefit from it.

In addition, he considered the cumulative effect of the theatre's nationwide reputation and the publicity Sullivan gets to be yet another positive economic influence.

The community lost all of that the year the theatre was dark. In addition to the negative publicity, according to Isaacs, the economic effect was palpable. "The town during the summer was relatively slow. The money wasn't spent here and, because of the multiplier effect, it impacted everybody. All this money spent has sales tax. The city lost revenue, the county lost revenue. It had impact across the board."

Isaacs asserted that during the season the theatre was closed, there was a drop in tax revenue for the city of Sullivan. There, in fact, does appear to have been a decrease in reported sales tax receipts in the associated areas for the relevant time frame. During the third quarter (July, August, and September), which corresponds most closely to the theatre season, sales tax revenue for drinking and eating places dropped by 13.5 percent between 1979 and 1980, when the theatre was closed. Conversely, between 1980 and 1981, when the theatre reopened, sales tax revenue increased for the same time period by almost 22 percent. The total third-quarter reported sales tax for the city of Sullivan, however, dropped by 18 percent between 1979 and 1981.

The economic significance of the theatre to the area remains a relevant and debatable issue. The theatre's broader and more ephemeral contributions to the community are what seemed to fuel the rescue efforts. Those involved were not so callow as to link the city's continued existence with the survival of the theatre. "Sullivan would go on [without theatre]," said Sharon White. "Kids would still go to school and the adults would still drive off to Decatur and Mattoon to their jobs, but there would be something missing. There is something that goes on here in the summertime. The town comes alive." Whether the summer of 1980 is being discussed in economic or cultural terms, the loss of the theatre created a void in Sullivan that many people wanted filled.

The Friends of The Little Theatre

In February 1981, business and civic leaders of Sullivan created the Friends of The Little Theatre. Memories exist where minutes do not that account for alternative stories of how the idea for the Friends was conceived. One story has the organization being inspired on the spur of the moment by the late Bob Best, the publisher of the *News-Progress,* during a telephone conversation with then Congressman Paul Simon, installing Sharon White as the group's first president. The Friends, consequently, convened in the Whites' living room. Simon said he remembered conversations with Best and others regarding keeping the theatre going but little beyond that.

According to another version, the idea of creating a nonprofit organization had been informally discussed among the key players until they finally met, again in the Whites' living room, with the late Reverend Stewart Rowles, minister of the First Presbyterian Church, elected as the president. Regardless of the origins of the Friends of The Little Theatre, the organization was able to keep The Little Theatre afloat, although they often wondered how.

The primary players in the Friends of The Little Theatre were Stewart and Pauline Rowles, Bob and Marion Best, Wayne and Patsy Jones, Richard and Jamie Isaacs, and Ron and Sharon White. A board of directors to oversee the operations of the theatre was formed from members of the Friends. Margaret Hollowell, who joined the board later that spring, said the Friends believed they had enough contacts among the people who had worked at the theatre under Little to put together a production staff. "The whole idea was just to keep the thing going. It was to be not-for-profit. We just didn't realize it was to be *so much* not-for-profit."

Several Friends members made sizable financial contributions, but involvement in the group was not conditional on financial resources, as Pauline Rowles pointed out.

> I think in any small town there is a group of people who are the shakers and movers. The same people seem to be involved in anything that is headed anywhere. Sullivan is no different. The people who comprised the Friends, except for Stew and I, were financially independent and upscale. They were part of the power base, financially and politically. They were accustomed to the things they were doing being successful. I can't quite figure out how we got there, but it was part of our social circle. It didn't have anything to do with how much money we had.

As Margaret Hollowell mentioned, the idea behind the creation of the Friends was to keep the theatre going. With the exception of Sharon White, who had done costumes for Guy Little, no one among the Friends had an insider's knowledge of running a theatre. What they lacked in experience, they made up for in willingness. As Rowles had observed, "We just sort of took a leap of faith."

The Friends hired two people from St. Louis, Jean Webster and Norbert Krausz, to produce. Webster and Krausz had both worked in Sullivan for Little in a number of capacities. The 1981 season opened on 10 July with *Same Time, Next Year* with Kathryn Hays. The season continued with a touring company of Don Brockett's *Big Bad Burlesque,* Rue McClanahan in *Butterflies Are Free,* Hans Conreid in *Never Too Late,* and an ensemble production of *Grease.*

The turnout was good enough to encourage the Friends to continue even though they wound up in the red by $2,000 or $3,000 at the season's end. In retrospect, Ron White said it should have been an omen. What they have since discovered is that nonprofit theatre is difficult and tends to operate at a deficit. "I think at that point in time we were young and naive in the business [and] thought we ought to even break even, at least. A theatre like that is never going to break even on its sales of tickets. It always needs subsidies from businesses and grants and donations from people."

The Friends continued to work with Webster and Krausz through the 1982 season but with less success. The omen White mentioned seems to have been missed by others as well. White said that during the first season they had a close-knit group that worked closely with both of the producers. During the second year, Krausz was not around and Webster was basically in charge. The Friends found some of her business practices inappropriate, so, as Ron White put it, "she disappeared." Margaret Hollowell was a bit more direct. Webster had apparently hidden unpaid bills and neglected to tell the Friends about the debt that was being accumulated.

The 1982 season produced one notable curiosity. The second production of the season was a three-week run of *Oklahoma!* with John Wesley Shipp, an actor from a soap opera. As of 1995, that show has remained the theatre's most attended production since 1982 with nearly eight thousand paid attendance.

The following year Tom Marks and Mike Wilson, both from Chicago, took over as producers. They also lasted two years. "Their concept of theatre," said Hollowell, "was to do smaller-scale shows than the previous manager wanted to do. That was okay up to a point, except nobody wanted to see the small-scale shows we were doing. In addition to which, we still thought we were tied to the star system and that was an enormously expensive mistake."

Pauline Rowles mirrored Hollowell's sentiments about the financial constraints of star theatre. "Artistically, I don't think anybody could fault the productions from the very beginning. It wasn't very many years until the star system wore itself out because those folks priced themselves out of the market—our market." The question became whether audiences would still attend because they were accustomed to productions with recognizable names and faces.

Between 1985 and 1987, The Little Theatre employed three more people working in a melange of business and artistic capacities, none with any notable success. During this time, Guy Little had returned to Sullivan from Milwaukee and had become active on the board, in part to help figure out where the theatre was heading. Also, at this time, Margaret Hollowell found herself president of the board, a situation she recalls sardonically.

The presidency of the board had rotated among most of the members when it was offered to Hollowell. She said she did not want it because she did not live in Sullivan. "They said, 'We don't care. We have had it up to here. You have to do this. . . . You have the best relationship with Guy of any of us and maybe we can get through this thing.' I was president probably 1985, 1986, and 1987. I know it was forever."

Among the responsibilities thrust upon her was firing one of the managers. According to Hollowell, the duty to sack the manager was left to her because the previous president, Bob Best, was too soft-hearted to do it. He did offer to write Hollowell a speech for the occasion. "I was a basket case because this was in the middle of the season. He was pretty surprised." The dismissal was effective immediately. When asked what the board did for the rest of the season, Hollowell replied, "Limped . . . and went big money in the hole."

It was at this point the board decided that, if the theatre was going to survive, they needed a professional manager, someone with a real business sense and not just artistic vision. The product of their 1987 national search was Leonard Anderson, who took over in January 1988.

CONSEQUENCES OF THE FRIENDS

When Anderson took the helm, he found himself in a leaking boat in the middle of the storm heading for uncharted waters. One major challenge he faced was the changing nature of the theatre business and the uncertain future of small theatres. This meant, for The Little Theatre at least, doing away with the star system and changing to a new type of contract with Equity. Another, much more localized mess he inherited was simply the overwhelming accumulation of debt. But with all of the red ink, Anderson also benefited from the salutary effects of the Friends' involvement with the theatre.

The primary consequence was, according to Sharon White, a feeling that the theatre now belonged to the community rather than to Guy Little, even though he still owned the building. Marilyn Stubblefield, who had pitched in during the theatre's first season, described the change as coming full circle. "There are a lot more people involved with the theatre itself . . . though, granted, not *that* many people. I think there's more a feeling of its the town's; before, it was Guy's."

Anderson would be central in changing the perception, as well as the reality, of who owned the theatre. The sentiment, however, of more people within the community embracing and identifying with the theatre had been evolving even before he got to town. Two events were largely responsible.

The creation of the Friends was instrumental in altering perceptions about the theatre. Although it was still being operated under the star system, having a collection of recognizable and identifiable community members who relied on volunteerism help spread the word of the theatre into wider and different circles. The declaration about the theatre actually had not changed much: It was, as it more or less had always been, how unique the existence of the theatre was, how good the productions were, and how wonderfully nice and unaffected the theatre people were. What had changed was who was listening.

Among long-time residents, there was a growing awareness of the actors and techies who came to town. Community members were getting to know people from the theatre as individuals rather than as "those showdogs." This growing awareness also occurred among members of the theatre board, a change Ron White described with self-effacing humor.

White described a time in the early to mid-1970s when some of the theatre people were at their most flamboyant and when the "showdog" image had peaked. White, whose wife had costumed for Little from the early 1970s and had only been vicariously involved through her activities, found himself feeling quite uncomfortable around some of the theatre people. He spoke specifically about one costume designer who "was one of the kindest, best people I have ever known." This person also was someone who "was out of the closet before people knew there was a closet," a characteristic that made White nervous. "I have to admit I was uncomfortable early on when we first moved to town and Sharon started working up there. Matthew would come around and I thought, 'Good night, I don't want to be around this guy. It might be contagious. . . .' I didn't know. I'm a good ol' redneck boy from Flora, Illinois, so I understand how people feel, a lot of them." With perceptions changing over time and as a result of more people becoming involved with the theatre, White believes attitudes like the one he formerly held have dissipated.

Ron White's involvement led into intense friendships with people from the theatre. "I really didn't get to know the people within the theatre until we started the Friends and then began to meet the actors and the techies and realized how they are family." White described one actor in particular who first appeared in 1981 and who "is like a brother." Jack Milo, a member of the company, came to town with his wife and nine-year-old daughter. White and his wife, and many others in town, watched Milo's daughter grow up and have followed the careers of Milo and his wife.

Other people have also developed the kind of connections described by White, which continue to evolve into very personal missions. Pauline Rowles found her involvement with the Friends allowed her to indulge in one of her favorite passions—cooking. According to Equity contract, if there are less than two hours between a matinee and evening performance, the theatre has to feed the Equity actors. "Our producers," said Rowles, "always felt like the whole company deserved a meal if it was going to be that short of a break." Rowles, along with her husband, began to feed people, and she continued after her husband's death in 1989. Rowles, who is active in other community organizations, is very frank about what she gets out of feeding the company. "I never had the least urge to perform, but like a lot of other people, I like to be recognized. I enjoy compliments. I get more than my share of that with my involvement with the theatre and the kids because it is so personal. It's such a joy for me to do, and I have met some of the nicest people doing this kind of stuff."

Emilee Best found a similar sense of satisfaction. Best became involved with the theatre quite by accident in 1983, the year after she moved to Sullivan from Chicago with her husband and son. The female lead of *Dames at Sea* discovered Best was a manicurist who did acrylic nails, and this contact led to Best getting to know people in the company. Over the years, Best's personal mission evolved into finding acceptable housing for the members of the company, especially the college interns. Sitting in the living room of a restored Victorian house, Best said, "As you can see, I think that your home is the most important place. . . . If you have the basic creature comforts, everything else comes easy after that. These kids did not have that."

The interns and apprentices used to live in a dilapidated house a couple of blocks from the theatre, infamous for its infestations. After that house was razed, Best helped find, clean, and furnish housing for the company members. "It's all ugly," she said jokingly of the furniture and housewares assembled through donations and rummage sales. "It's all seventies harvest gold and avocado green. But the kids like it and it's clean and it's decent housing. [And] they don't fight mice or rats or roaches."

The second transformative event during the first part of the Friends' reign had a more widespread and residual effect on the community.

Its impact on the theatre, however, is a bit more speculative. In 1982, for the first time, the Sullivan High School musical was performed at The Little Theatre instead of the high school gym. Although Guy Little had hired high school students during the first few seasons and over the years an endless supply of teenage girls worked as ushers, the theatre and the school system never established any sort of partnership or collaboration. This remained the case even after the high school resurrected its annual musical in the mid-1970s with *Oklahoma!* In addition, Sullivan High School had always had respectable band and chorus programs, though they could never be described as stellar.

In 1981, David Fehr was hired to fill the vocal music position at the high school. He said he applied for the job in part because he had been to the theatre as a child to see *Peter Pan*. He personally became involved with the theatre by playing the piano in the pit for *Grease*. With the help and support of Bob and Marion Best, Fehr used the theatre for the 1982 high school musical, *The Sound of Music*. According to Sharon White, who described this new chorus teacher as "bold as brass and still is," the reason Fehr was able to do the high school musical in the theatre was because he asked, something nobody had done before.

When he first moved to town, Fehr was told that the theatre was not really accepted by the community. "Having the high school musical in the theatre got townspeople through the doors, and let them see their children on the same stage as the 'stars.'" He went on to say he hoped it helped break down some of the myths and misconceptions that existed about the theatre. The following year Fehr did *The King and I* and cast John Dwyer, a sophomore football player, as the king. Dwyer and the two other boys who played the king's bodyguards all shaved their heads for the roles. From that point, said Fehr, it was okay for boys to be in the musicals.

Under Fehr, the high school show choir blossomed. "The theatre helped the school music program because, as we traveled and competed with the Sullivan Singers, people knew of The Little Theatre On The Square," said Fehr. "It was easier to build pride and a sense of history into the group that also performed on the same stage." The Singers went on to win two national titles.

Fehr continued with the theatre during the summers until 1993 when he took a new teaching position in Clinton, Mississippi. The high school musicals are still done in the theatre, and people who would not otherwise set foot into the theatre do go to watch their children and grandchildren on stage. For some, according to Sharon White, they finally learn "it's just a theatre, it's not hell, there isn't a satanic ritual going on in here. It's just a theatre."

During the decade between Guy Little's exit and Leonard Anderson's entrance, The Little Theatre experienced a profound range of extremes, except, that is, for matters of finances, which went in only one direction. Among the reasons Little had left was the cost of doing star theatre. Subsequent producers discovered the same problem to the point of being forced to cancel a season for financial reasons. The potential loss of the theatre inspired community members to form a nonprofit organization and keep it going. At one end, the Friends of The Little Theatre began to get community members involved with the theatre, spreading the idea that it belonged to the community rather than to an individual or family. At the other, they faced the same fiscal nightmares as did their predecessors. The constant struggle to keep the theatre open would lead to a reorganization and reexamination of the theatre's role within the community and region.

Bob Crane, photographed with apprentices, starred in *Beginner's Luck* in 1971. (Courtesy David W. Mobley)

Apprentices relax in front of the rehearsal hall on the east side of the square in 1971. (Courtesy David W. Mobley)

Set designer Bob Soule *(center)*, photographed with apprentices in 1971, was known for his elaborate sets and stage design. (Courtesy David W. Mobley)

Margaret Hamilton *(left)* and Ann Miller costarred in *Blithe Spirit* in 1973. (Courtesy David W. Mobley)

Ann Miller facing upstage in 1973. (Courtesy David W. Mobley)

Harve Presnell starred in *On a Clear Day You Can See Forever* in 1973. (Courtesy David W. Mobley)

Bill Hayes, with costar in *The Fantasticks* in 1973, appeared at The Little Theatre four times between 1969 and 1976. (Courtesy David W. Mobley)

Lesley Ann Warren starred in *Irma La Douce* in 1973. (Courtesy David W. Mobley)

Feature photograph from the *Moultrie County News* in 1974 promoting *Hair* before the production became controversial. (Courtesy David W. Mobley)

The main players from *Hair* in 1974. (Courtesy David W. Mobley)

The Tribe, or cast, from *Hair* in 1974. Toward the end of the controversy over the production, the cast was invited to an area church to repent. (Courtesy David W. Mobley)

Leonard Nimoy starred in *One Flew over the Cuckoo's Nest* in 1974. (Courtesy David W. Mobley)

Isabel Sanford, who appeared with Lillian Lehman in *And Mama Makes Three* in 1977, was the only African American to star at The Little Theatre. (Courtesy David W. Mobley)

Stubby Kaye starred in *Fiddler on the Roof* in 1977. (Courtesy David W. Mobley)

Charles Bell *(right)* and Shannon McHugh were featured in *Seven Brides for Seven Brothers* in 1988. (Courtesy R. R. Best)

Glen Washington with the cast of *Joseph and the Amazing Technicolor Dreamcoat* in 1988. (Courtesy R. R. Best)

Artistic director M. Seth Reines *(left)* with Jeff Talbott and Jack Milo *(right)* in 1988. (Courtesy R. R. Best)

Executive director Leonard Anderson *(left)* made a rare stage appearance in *Carousel* in 1994. (Courtesy R. R. Best)

The cast of *West Side Story* in 1992. (Courtesy R. R. Best)

Jack Milo *(left)* appeared with Michael Haws in *A Funny Thing Happened on the Way to the Forum* in 1996. (Courtesy R. R. Best)

6

THE MORE THINGS CHANGE

Leonard Anderson's tenure as manager of the theatre started the current phase of The Little Theatre's existence. From 1981 to 1987, the theatre had endured seven people functioning in a pastiche of positions, with the whole enterprise overseen by a board of directors primarily composed of people from the Friends of the Little Theatre. Under Anderson and M. Seth Reines, hired as artistic director in 1988, the theatre found a stability and direction it had been lacking since 1978, Guy S. Little Jr.'s final season. Working conjointly and individually, Anderson and Reines brought a consistency and professionalism to the productions while maintaining an awareness of the attitudes of Sullivan residents.

Despite this cognizance, Anderson and Reines's reign has not been without tribulation. Each has experienced the specter of theatre seasons past, albeit quite differently. For Anderson, whose responsibilities include fund raising and financial management, the battle to keep the theatre afloat became a political issue when the question of funding came before the Sullivan City Council. Consequently, the refractory nature of the subject resurfaced, revealing quite unaltered and, in some cases, archaic opinions, particularly when juxtaposed with the theatre's changing role within the community and region.

Reines, on the other hand, had to confront, in a more direct manner, the "showdog" image. As artistic director, Reines cast every show and advised Anderson on hiring of other company personnel, especially recommending artistic staff. He experienced the effects of memories held by community members, something that directly influenced his casting decisions.

But for everything Anderson and Reines did to reconcile the existence of The Little Theatre in a community like Sullivan, they still ran into many of the same issues and problems that appeared when Guy Little first opened the theatre in 1957. Although much had changed, a few things remained quite constant, including the rift between urban and rural lifestyles and the very basic dilemma of where to house outsiders in a community not acculturated to doing so.

Leonard Anderson and the Pursuit of Money

In addition to the accumulated debt of many years, Anderson also inherited the theatre in its poststar years. The star system had essentially priced itself out of the market of small theatres. The Little Theatre had featured star performers through the end of the 1984 season, operating under a standard contract with Actors Equity Association. In 1985, the theatre switched to a Small Professional Theatre (SPT) contract, taking advantage of a new contract category created by Equity in 1984.

The idea of the SPT designation was twofold. One expectation was that more theatres would begin as small Equity companies and grow into full Equity contracts. A second objective was to increase employment for union members living outside major metropolitan areas, even if at a lower pay scale. A byproduct of the new contract was that it allowed small legitimate houses to survive and flourish as fully professional theatres. This was (and remains) the contract under which The Little Theatre operated when Anderson was hired.

Anderson was one of approximately sixty people who responded to a national search for a general manager. He had been the managing director of the Black Hills Playhouse, a non-Equity, university-sponsored summer theatre program in South Dakota. He said he took the job in Sullivan because of the history and national reputation of The Little Theatre. "I accepted the job because I saw a theatre that had changed from a commercial venture to a nonprofit venture and I saw a lot of challenge," he said. The question remains whether Anderson anticipated the bulk of the challenges that would quickly come his way.

According to Pauline Rowles, Anderson made quite an impression on the board. "I remember very clearly the day the Friends met Leonard. I think there was a collective sigh of relief. Here was somebody who was not going to run up monstrous amounts of travel bills, bringing in friends. He was not going to say stupid things. We had not had any type of business management early on, and there we sat with all this debt." Anderson, Rowles continued, came in as a businessman, a fact the business people on the board appreciated. "They had a feeling he knew what he was doing."

Margaret Hollowell, a member of the selection committee that also included Guy Little, recalled talking to the chairman of the board at the Black Hills Playhouse about Anderson. She was told that he would drown the board of The Little Theatre in facts and figures and charts, that he would have everything so figured out the board would never know what hit them. "Sure enough," Hollowell said, "he has. The point is he had the handle we did not have. He had the financial handle."

Anderson was hired as general manager, and in 1995 his title was changed to executive director. As noted, he assumed the role as a businessman—something other businesspeople on the board and in Sullivan could understand—even though the theatre had become a nonprofit enterprise. This change in fiscal status was something many people could not understand, and spreading the word became one of Anderson's missions. Because the theatre had operated as a commercial venture for so many years, he said the public has had a hard time understanding that it is nonprofit and subsequently needs and, in fact, qualifies for grants and donations to survive. "We have made great, great, great strides in re-educating the community. . . . But there are still some people who consider us to be 'just another business,' and why should we help you out any more than we would help out a local car dealership?"

Such an attitude did not necessarily affect the grants the theatre has received from traditional funding sources. These include programs sponsored by the Illinois Arts Council (IAC), and the Illinois Department of Commerce and Community Affairs (DCCA). The problems came when Anderson appealed to local and area businesses, especially those unfamiliar with the theatre or knowing it only by reputation. "The majority of the people who consider the theatre to be 'just another business' aren't interested in the theatre as an art form," said Anderson. "They could care less. They don't come to the productions. They don't recognize the economic impact the theatre has on the community because they probably do not derive any personal economic benefit." He continued to say the same people fail to realize they do benefit because the theatre makes a $1.5 million contribution to the local economy.

The theatre did, in fact, receive a good bit in grant money before Anderson was hired; he simply took the pursuit of money more seriously and aggressively. Between 1982 and 1990, The Little Theatre received almost $250,000 in a combination of tourism, marketing, and annual subsidies from DCCA and IAC. This amount includes a 1986 $100,000 grant from DCCA's Illinois Small Business Development Program awarded to the City of Sullivan to renovate the theatre. Guy Little still owned the theatre building and leased it to the Friends of The Little Theatre.

During this time, certain individuals among the Friends were still supporting the theatre with their own money. Ron White, a member of the board and financial backer, described the emotional and personal efforts taken to keep the theatre going. White said he was probably one of the more stubborn ones on the board, who did not want to see the theatre go under and who felt responsible for holding on so tightly as the theatre went deeper into debt. Consequently, he and two others took their theatre-saving efforts one step further. "We guaranteed the loan to the Friends of The Little Theatre to keep operating. That would have been a three-year accumulation of red ink and, by then, the people would have been saying no more credit until you pay us. It gets to that stage periodically." Things got to that stage again just after Anderson moved to Sullivan.

THE THEATRE POLITICIZED

Leonard Anderson's first season with The Little Theatre was 1988, which, he said, went pretty well. "Within six months," he said, "I realized the theatre was in a lot more financial trouble than I had been led to believe." Still, attendance for the season was good, and, despite the financial difficulties the theatre faced, "we were able to kind of maintain an even keel."

The following year, however, matters were much more disheartening. Attendance was down dramatically, and the season ended in the red. This, said Anderson, "coupled with the existing debt that I inherited; it appeared that it was all over. We honestly felt we may have to close."

Anderson realized that keeping the theatre going would require direction and feedback from more people than just the existing board. "At that time, the board was seven or nine people," said Anderson. "Most of them had been involved since the founding of the non-profit corporation in 1981, and they were tired. Several of them had been involved financially to the extent they were drained out."

In addition to debt and the exhaustion of the existing board of directors, Anderson had also inherited some negative public relation images that hampered his search for money. During his first couple of years, he said he would go into local businesses and be on the receiving end of a lecture about how the theatre did not pay its bills. This feeling carried over to the members of the board who were also held responsible. Anderson said he realized things needed to change.

He pulled together an ad hoc committee, what he called a "concerned citizens committee," consisting of local theatre supporters and subscription ticket holders. They helped him get in touch with state senator Penny Severns, who got the theatre a ninety-thousand-dollar line item in the proposed state budget. "Had it passed, it would have come directly to the theatre to help us. Unfortunately, the governor that year vetoed $4.5 million worth of what he considered to be pork and, although he didn't single out our ninety thousand dollars, it was part of what he vetoed."

Because they could not get money at the state level, they took their plea to the City of Sullivan for financial support. The theatre did get its money, but what Anderson ambivalently described as "a considerable amount of discussion and finagling" was actually a revealing example of small-town politics.

Ron White was a member of the Sullivan City Council when Anderson made his request for financial support in late 1989. White could not vote on the issue without a conflict of interest because his wife, Sharon, was still a member of the theatre's board of directors. White said he did advocate Anderson's cause among the council members.

White said Anderson visited each member with his economic

impact facts and figures, and "everybody—some quicker than others—decided maybe it was a good thing that the city should support the theatre monetarily." Anderson had also gone to Mayor Tom Dean, who, according to White, had apparently told Leonard he would support it.

Anderson, optimistic about the outcome, appeared at the council meeting with what White described as "great joy and anticipation in his eyes." The issue, however, did not pass because, while White abstained and the other council members voted "yes," the mayor changed his vote to "no." "I think it was kind of a political thing on his part. Apparently he had gotten—"scared" is the wrong word—he just had second thoughts. If he voted for this thing, it might mean that he would not be reelected. It was a long way to reelection time, too. He still had two years to go. Somebody had said something to Tom to make him change his mind."

White said he took the defeat of the proposal personally and spent several days wondering what could be done. Because the issue was a financial matter, it required a four-fifths vote of the council and because he abstained, everyone else had to vote "yes" in order for it to pass. The key became figuring out a way to enable White to vote.

White decided that if the three other council members would continue with their votes, White and his wife would sever any ties they had with the theatre, making him eligible to vote. "We went to the bank and borrowed several thousand dollars to pay off our portion of the note that we had guaranteed. So that was clear. [Sharon] resigned from the board of the theatre so we were clear there. Then I talked to the city attorney and he called the state's attorney, and we followed his guidance." A week later, White called a special council meeting to recall the issue and vote again. This time the funding passed because White was able to vote even though the mayor still voted "no."

The theatre got a total of seventy-five thousand dollars from the city; sixty thousand was an outright, one-time grant with an additional fifteen thousand presented as a challenge grant. The challenge grant, said Anderson, was originally proposed as a one-to-one match. Instead, Anderson agreed to raise two dollars for each one of the city's fifteen thousand dollars, an effort he said would make the board work harder and show a greater commitment.

The consequences of the theatre's appeal to the city for support were twofold. In January 1990, the theatre underwent a total reorganization. The name of the nonprofit corporation was changed from the Friends of The Little Theatre, Inc., to The Little Theatre On The Square, Inc. The local board of directors of less than a dozen members was expanded to a regional board of trustees with upwards of forty-eight people from half a dozen central Illinois counties.

Part of the decision behind the reorganization was to get fresh blood onto the board, including people who had not previously been associated with the theatre. Lynn Elder, a Sullivan resident and an executive at A. E. Staley Manufacturing Company in Decatur, succeeded Margaret Hollowell as president of the board. Among those also named to the board were Dick Burcham, a vice president of the First National Bank in Sullivan, and Robert Corley, a Sullivan business owner.

Emilee Best, who also served on the board, said she noticed a big change in attitudes when Elder and Corley took over the board. "They had credibility. They were not theatre people." Margaret Hollowell, who had been replaced by Elder as the board president, noticed very similar changes following the reorganization. "Businessmen don't have time to lose money. It's just theatre nuts [that do]. . . . They weren't about to tolerate expensive salaries when people weren't performing or drawing." She continued to say that many of the new people on the board had connections to large, area corporations, like ADM and Staley, that might, and eventually did, give money to theatre, something that had been impossible before.

A second consequence of the city giving money to the theatre was increased discussion about the theatre, revealing some very deep-seated opinions. A council member's affirmative vote to fund the theatre was not indicative of support for the theatre. Ron White recalled that one of the council members took pride in the fact that he had never stepped into the theatre. White, quite bluntly, said, "Pardon my English, but I think he was afraid that if he went through that front door, his balls would fall off. There are just some good ol' redneck boys like that around this town. It's unfortunate, but it's the way it is."

White summed up observations made by many. "My own thoughts are that it was operated by the Littles for so many years, they still have it tied to the Littles. They still look at it as a privately owned and operated entity, and that if they are donating to the theatre, they are somehow giving money to the Littles."

In some cases, this attitude went beyond The Little Theatre, extending to the Little family and grudges that have been held since the 1930s. At that time, Guy Little Sr. managed for an insurance company several farms that had been foreclosed. A frequently expressed local sentiment, however, was that the land was essentially stolen. Consequently, many of those people who maintained this belief would not have anything to do with the theatre.

Even among those people who realized that the theatre was no longer subsidized by Little family money, many believed that taxpayer money should not be used to subsidize a business they perceived to be no different from any other. Richard Isaacs, who became a theatre board member after the reorganization, said the city council appeared to take a lot of heat because of the decision to support the theatre. The attitude among those disagreeing was that if their businesses have to survive without "free money," so should the theatre.

"I think I caught more heat than the other guys because people knew what I did," said Ron White. "They didn't know exactly how much, but they knew I had done something to allow myself the opportunity to vote on that issue." He also said his business was affected by some people who could not separate his actions as city councilman from his role as pharmacist.

White suspected the theatre became an issue when he ran for reelection in 1991. Originally unopposed, his seat as commissioner of accounts and finances was challenged by the city clerk, a man White speaks of with much respect. His challenger did much door-to-door campaigning, while White took a more serendipitous approach to the election. White wound up winning by eight votes, and his opponent did not demand a recount.

The theatre's board of trustees approached the city council again in 1993 to get financial support, even just forgiveness of utilities. White said at that time he encountered another commissioner "who hadn't been to the theatre and wasn't about to [go]." Even after White took this council member to a children's production to see the effect the theatre had on parts of the community, he still was not ready to commit city money to support it.

In 1991, The Little Theatre On The Square, Inc., received forty thousand dollars in the form of a tourism attraction grant administered through the Illinois Department of Commerce and Community Affairs to go toward the purchase of the theatre from Guy Little. Prior to that, Little had been leasing the theatre to the nonprofit corporation for a dollar a year. Since the purchase of the theatre, the corporation has made a number of capital improvements, including purchase of the building next door for the ticket office in 1992 and installation of a heating and air conditioning system in the theatre and dressing rooms in 1995 and 1996.

THEATRE IN THE CORNFIELDS—ACT TWO

When The Little Theatre stopped featuring stars, a frequently expressed sentiment among some theatergoers was that the theatre would lose its appeal. This fact was lost on neither Leonard Anderson nor Seth Reines. Instead of placing emphasis on one person, both believed the focus should be on the entire production. "If you have Mickey Rooney on the stage," said Anderson, "you don't have to pay as much attention to costumes and sets and the other aspects of the production. From the beginning, I have striven for high quality in all aspects of the whole operation, because if we don't have a good product we can't expect people to pay money to see it."

Similarly, Reines considered consistency as crucial as overall quality, even if that meant being limited in choice of production. Using *Who's Afraid of Virginia Woolf?* as an example, he said the theatre under Guy Little "did dramatically more exciting things" than they could do now because the audience in those days went primarily to see a star. Often, however, the shows lacked consistency. "In some cases, the physical productions were very good, and in some cases, the standards were not nearly as high. We cannot give them stars, nor do I want to, but it means that we have to provide exciting physical productions with good casts so that [there's] another reason for them coming back."

Many people would say that what Reines and Anderson were doing, putting together "exciting physical productions with good casts," more than made up for The Little Theatre not featuring stars. Reines had begun hiring a handful of people who returned to Sullivan on a semiregular basis, if not annually. "I frequently said we began growing our own stars," said Pauline Rowles. "We began having people who had caught the audience's eye and interest. We had those people back and, by the third or fourth year, people were coming to see the performers, not necessarily the plays, just as they were doing when we had the stars . . . on a much smaller scale, of course."

According to Chuck Bell, there are people who would say The Little Theatre *is* doing star theatre: "Jack Milo is a star." Bell goes on to say that there is a much larger group who would say Milo is not a star because he has never been on television. The debate over what qualifies one as a star was complicated by Jack Milo's appearance in the movie *That Thing You Do*. "All of these people have turned around and are saying, 'He's made it, he's made it.' Jack's done several films, just not one with a decent role."

The point remains, Reines and Anderson, but primarily the former, have been putting together groups of people that, as Reines puts it, make theatre in Sullivan "sort of a rep company," especially among the Equity actors. He knew what to expect from the actors and could start selecting shows that accentuated individual's talents. "Casting starts in my head almost immediately," said Reines. "*Will Rogers Follies* was selected [for the 1996 season] because of Michael Haws. I knew he would be wonderful in it." This practice worked for people who were familiar with Sullivan and The Little Theatre. The other side of the same scenario is that Reines had to attract people who would not only want to spend a summer in the corn belt, but people who would fit in the corn belt.

SHOWDOGS REVISITED

There is no doubt that attitudes in Sullivan about The Little Theatre have changed. For one thing, the term "showdog" now is used euphemistically and jokingly among the theatre company rather than pejoratively against them by residents. Many more people from the area are involved with the theatre, and there is a familiarity between community members and theatre folks as individuals instead of a group. But for all the things that have changed, many attitudes have not. Seth Reines, Leonard Anderson, company members, and even local supporters continue to run into the collective residue of long memories in a small town as they go about their business.

Among Reines's primary responsibilities as artistic director have been recruiting and casting. Any given season is generally announced during the last production of the preceding season. The Artistic Committee, a subcommittee of the theatre board, comes up with a list of possible productions; Reines does the same. From the total possibilities, they decide on eight or nine that, during the fourth show, they let the audience members vote on. Reines said this process gives Anderson, the board, and himself an idea of the direction the audience members want to see the theatre take. "It does make the audience feel like they're involved in the selection process. We want to do everything we can to make them feel like it's their theatre." In addition, Reines has to make the season enticing enough to attract potential cast members, all the while knowing that they can make dramatically more than $125–$175 a week performing in productions in theme parks or on cruise ships.

Once a season is selected, auditions usually occur in January or February, which includes large regional auditions where several stock companies are represented. "There is one in St. Louis called the Midwest Auditions, and between forty and fifty companies come together there and see, within two days, five hundred people. Then we have Equity auditions in Chicago once a year, sometimes in St. Louis. It has a lot to do with the people that I have worked with in other venues over the years."

According to The Little Theatre's contract with Equity, the theatre must maintain a minimum of four Equity actors for each production, as well as an Equity stage manager. The Equity actors are in addition to nonunion professional actors, college interns, and high school apprentices, and a limited number of child actors. According to the 1996 IAC final report, a total of sixty-eight people were employed by the theatre, twenty-six in the acting company.

Through the spring, Reines puts together the artistic and technical staff and starts planning the specifics of the season, so that by Memorial Day weekend, when the artistic and technical staffs start arriving in Sullivan, they can start building the show. "What happens is you put together a season with a flow sheet of who is playing what role all the way through and then it changes ten times. It's always fun to come here at the beginning of the summer and see actually what your final mix is because it has nothing to do with what it started from."

The company is limited by Equity to fifty rehearsal hours to get a show up, said Reines. Each show opens on a Wednesday and by the following Thursday, they start rehearsing the next production. The interns and apprentices rehearse the children's shows in the mornings, and on days with matinees, there are only two hours for rehearsing the next main-stage show. The pace at which a season moves affects the type of people Reines hires. "Some people work really well if they have a long rehearsal period. We don't have that. I need actors who have fast memorization skills, people who can pick up dance quickly."

In addition to looking for people who have the requisite artistic skills, Reines also looks for people who will work well together and fit in with the community. He considers both essential because, just as when a season is being planned and he has to appeal to both actors and audience members, it is fundamental to keep both groups coming back. "We try to do everything within reason to make [the actors] enjoy their experience and feel good about the work they do." This, Reines said, creates good word-of-mouth advertising and makes it easier for him to recruit people from year to year.

Equally important is keeping in mind the mores of the community. This is something that, according to Reines, was not done in past years, evidenced by resistance among community residents when he first got to Sullivan. He recalled one encounter in particular with a local woman in the laundromat who made it quite clear she did not want the theatre people in town. When Reines asked why, the woman replied, "We remember."

"[There have been] a few isolated incidents but it was remembering the sixties and seventies," said Reines. "And anybody who has ever said anything to me, I just say 'Since I have been here, men have not walked down the street holding hands or there hasn't been nude sunbathing on the courthouse lawn.' Whether that ever really happened or not, who knows?"

Reines said he has actually not hired certain people because their flamboyance may not fit in with Sullivan residents. He also makes sure the members of the company know they will be very visible. "Lenny and I have worked very, very hard. At the beginning of each season, we sit down with the company and say 'Hey, we don't care what you do in private. But, you are a member of this community and it's important that you respect them.'" Michael Haws, an Equity actor who grew up in Moultrie County, attributed this practice, in part, to an increased feeling of community acceptance.

Unless a theatre is in a major metropolitan area, Reines said, it is not unusual that the surrounding area will be a little more conservative than the summer stock company. "I would think that any community is going to be a little more conservative than the theatre people who come into it." Reines described a situation in Cumberland County, Tennessee, where the difference between the company members and locals was so extreme the actors' physical safety was threatened. Such problems do not exist in Moultrie County.

The major way in which the difference between residents and company members currently manifests itself in Sullivan is the split along rural-urban lines, something people observed about the theatre during its first season. Many people mentioned that the theatre brought elements of the city into Sullivan, whether it was an urban liberalism or types of behavior considered extreme. Even company members the first season, as noted in the 6 September 1957 *Moultrie County News,* commented about the lack of places to find food after performances and rehearsals.

Company members experienced in 1996 a rift between expectations, based on urban experiences, of what they thought they would find in Sullivan and what they actually found. Chuck Bell, a veteran of many summer stock seasons in out-of-the-way places, said some company members came from St. Louis and Chicago and expected to find night life or just a hamburger at three A.M.

> The town moves at a different pace; the rules are different and it is [the residents'] town. We do tell [the company members] at the beginning of the season: "Here is Sullivan, here are the rules. The bars close at this time. There's no liquor sales on Sunday. They will ticket your car if you park [all night on the square]. The trains are always ten-minute ordeals so if you see a train coming don't try to beat it, just get used to the fact you are going to be ten minutes late." You can say that 'til you are blue in the face, but until they experience it, they don't listen.

Some of the company members, said Bell, just do not fit in. He described a fellow with a pierced chest as an example. "He can't figure out why everybody thinks it's odd. I have said to him several times. 'What you have to do is go into the Spot and have breakfast and look at the people there. Then stand in front of the mirror and look at yourself and see what the difference is.'" Bell went on to say that the company members have an unusual position in the community. They are visitors, yet they have to live in Sullivan for the summer. "When you put together a company, you've got to have people who cannot only live together and work together and get along and have the right chemistry, you also have to incorporate that company with the community's chemistry."

Michael Haws heard both sides of the localite-cosmopolite debate. As a Chicago-based actor, he shared the city perspective with many of the actors, including a few who looked down at a corn town. He also had a fondness for Sullivan to the point that he would announce at the beginning of the season that it was his hometown. His dichotomous role actually enabled him to hear what the locals were saying. "With my family in the area," said Haws, "I get to hear all of the rumors and gossip going around about the theatre. My mother told me she heard some actors trashed a place where they were staying that had a swimming pool. I figured out that it was the opening night party at the country club where the actors were loud, left trash by the pool area, and stayed longer than [invited]."

Haws was not the only one privy to both perspectives. Emilee Best moved to Sullivan from Chicago in 1982 and got to know the theatre company the following summer. She could empathize with many members of the company and the culture shock they experienced being thrown into a different world with one stoplight and few places that stayed opened late.

Best also heard what Sullivan residents said about the theatre—some, in fact, warned her not to get involved—even though she considered the theatre to be Sullivan's distinguishing characteristic. "What was really fascinating to me was the attitude the people in this town had about the theatre people. It was like these two different worlds and we were warned not to get involved with the theatre people." She ascribed such a reaction to homophobia, an attitude to which she had been exposed while working in the beauty industry.

One of the reasons she thought she was warned not to get involved with the theatre was because "I guess we were what they considered prominent." Best's husband was an optometrist, and consequently, people in town expected a certain kind of attitude and behavior. "Down here when you are a doctor, they think you are really important. When we lived up near Chicago, we lived with steel workers. They didn't care what we did for a living. People down here were just so protective. . . . They would tell stories [about the theatre] . . . I mean this bizarre stuff. It was really fascinating. It was almost like, gosh, I don't fit in here anyplace but I really loved hearing all this."

Best was able to use another quality, that of an instant credibility she found attributed to social prominence, to her advantage as she became involved with finding housing for the theatre company. Finding housing of any kind for the company had been a problem for The Little Theatre since the first season. Sullivan could never be described as a tourist mecca, but accommodations then were even scarcer. Guy Little, in fact, advertised in the classified section of *Moultrie County News* for sleeping accommodations for cast members. Once he began featuring stars, he relied on friends like the Palmers to house those with top billing while the apprentices were relegated to the infested "intern house." Housing was still a problem when Leonard Anderson and Seth Reines were hired. The intern house had been torn down in the early 1980s and, at least for the 1988 season, some of the company members were put up in the Hotel Milroy, known locally as the "Hotel Mildew."

Securing housing was severely complicated by the lingering reputation of previous theatre people as tenants, perpetuated in the same manner as other scandalous stories in a small town. Pauline Rowles recalled a comment she had heard regarding new apartments being built in town. She said to the builder that she wished they could have been built years ago because there were never enough places to rent in Sullivan and the theatre could have used them. The builder's comment to her was "Well, not with their reputation." "I had to really bite my tongue because all these years we have worked so hard for the acceptance of the company. . . . It really disappointed me to hear that and I must have got a funny look on my face because the builder said, 'It takes a long time for a reputation to go away.' Now, really. As I say, I can't speak for anybody else . . . for the effect the theatre has had on anybody else. Some people are just never going to accept the idea that it's a worthwhile project."

Emilee Best ran into similar attitudes from property owners. In some cases, an owner would not rent to the theatre but they would rent to her. That was the only way the theatre had access to the house they called "Big Blue," an old funeral home a block east of the theatre. "I had credibility because there is the theatre group in town and then there are the town people. I was able to cross that bridge quite a bit when people saw that Tom and I were involved." At the end of the season, Best would make sure each apartment was left as it was found. She said there have been no problems and the company members have had decent places to live.

In many ways, the theatre has returned to its starting point in its forty-year existence. During its first few seasons, theatre people invaded Sullivan and found limited places to sleep, eat, and spend their few extra minutes when not working. Local people pitched in behind the scenes, painting sets, sewing costumes, doing whatever was necessary to keep the season running. Decades later, theatre people still invade Sullivan. They find a few more places, though still limited, to sleep and eat, and do not really need to look for anything to occupy their free time because they have so little of it anyway. Local people are still pitching in wherever and whenever needed but now usually cooking or cleaning apartments instead of painting sets.

With Leonard Anderson and Seth Reines at the helm, the theatre did indeed go full circle, if only to more comfortably and more securely reacclimatize the theatre to the community. That, however, has not been their only objective. In spite of apparent similarities, much has changed. When Guy Little opened the theatre in 1957, there was a build-it-and-they-will-come novelty to the whole enterprise, and attracting audiences rested largely on the shoulders of a star. Forty-plus years later, the theatre, like many other such organizations, faces an aging and disappearing audience base, and the need to attract new patrons (and new money) in some ways restructures the priorities of a theatre organization.

At the same time, Sullivan is facing a restructuring of its own. In 1957, Sullivan was a self-sustained and sufficient community. Around the time the theatre became a nonprofit organization and really started grappling for money, Sullivan was losing some of its autonomy, becoming a bedroom community with residents dependent on larger, distant cities for some very basic needs. It would, therefore, appear that the futures of the theatre and Sullivan are, in many ways, dependent on each other, their paths inextricably linked as they have been from the beginning, whether it is recognized or not.

CONCLUSION: THE THEATRE AS
MYTH AND REALITY

━━╍╍╍ᘓᘓᘓᘓ╍╍╍━━

The Little Theatre On The Square celebrated its fortieth season during the summer of 1997. The number of season attendees went beyond the expected twenty-four thousand. The festivities garnered a good bit of attention and fanfare, especially surrounding the production of *Brigadoon,* which occurred during the Fourth of July weekend, the anniversary of the opening of the first production of *Brigadoon* in Sullivan. The production even included Paul Barry, the first actor to set foot on the stage in 1957. The early years were remembered, along with recognition of the institution's unique status and veneration of the vision and perseverance of theatre founder Guy S. Little Jr. The celebrations, however, did not include past stars as had previous notable anniversaries. Nor was there an attempt to ignite nostalgia for the star years beyond the context of a particular evening's revelry.

The glamour and celebrity of the early years is certainly still part of the theatre's lore, but it is a waning part of the theatre's significance. The role of The Little Theatre within the community over its forty-plus years has changed, and with it is the role of associated memories and stories. The theatre evolved from a childhood dream of its founder to a star-studded, one-of-a-kind tourist attraction, to a more prosaic and resolute business enterprise. At each step, as different people were involved, the theater came to represent something distinct to each individual. Accordingly, how the theatre was remembered by those people and the place it had in their stories reaffirmed the theatre's latest metamorphosis.

Memory is, after all, a collective phenomenon, and as Arthur Neal (1998) pointed out, not static. Memories of specific events, both good and bad, are constantly being renegotiated to fit present circumstances. This is particularly true over time as later generations confront the problems unique to their time and, consequently, reevaluate the events and decisions made by the preceding generations. Guy Little's original mission may have varied little during his tenure, but as other people became involved, they adopted their own missions, forever altering the collective meaning of the theatre.

The Little Theatre's transformation did not occur in a vacuum. The business of theatre nationwide was changing, and Sullivan followed those trends. It was not that the present management did not want to be connected with the theatre's past; they could not if they expected to accomplish their missions for the theatre.

One of the primary changes the theatre experienced was in the originating sources of its major funding. Instead of a profit-making enterprise that relied on ticket sales and private investment, The Little Theatre is now a nonprofit organization funded largely by grants and donated money. Ticket sales are still vital; The Little Theatre, then and now, is expected to produce audience-pleasing shows. The current emphasis on grant money, especially coming from government and public sources, creates a more acute climate for greater accountability by the theatre to the community.

In April 1996, The Little Theatre On The Square was designated an Established Regional Arts Institution (ERAI) by the IAC for the 1997 fiscal year. Of the thirty-nine arts institutions statewide to receive such a designation, The Little Theatre was one of six producing theatres named and the only one in downstate Illinois. The creation of the ERAI program, according to a 1996 IAC press release, was intended to highlight significant cultural institutions throughout the state, and consideration for inclusion was based on six criteria, including regional significance, evidence of strong community support, financial stability, and a successful IAC funding history.

The Little Theatre's designation as a regional arts institution meant a substantial increase in IAC funding. The recognition from a statewide organization also acts as a stamp of legitimacy, raising the theatre to a status higher than just a local or area institution. As a result, the theatre could potentially attract the attention of people who otherwise had not taken notice. The downside to the same legitimizing process is that, because it is now acknowledged at the state level, some skeptics may believe that the theatre is no longer in need of local attention and funds, which is very much not the case.

The business of nonprofit professional theatre is unpredictable, but all things considered, The Little Theatre seems to be heading into a promising future. The same cannot be said for the city of Sullivan. A primary premise of this study is that the theatre, especially during its early years, altered perceptions and expectations of life within a small Midwestern community by creating a cultural time warp. The issue facing Sullivan is now much more fundamental: How is the community going to prevent getting stuck in a time rut?

Over the past decade or so, a once self-sufficient, if not economically vibrant, small town has become little more than a bedroom community for Mattoon, Decatur, and even Champaign-Urbana. The business district surrounding the courthouse square that twenty years ago housed prosperous local businesses is now dominated by closed storefronts and, as Alan Ehrenhalt (1996) describes, "occupied vacancies"—antique shops and other low-energy businesses.

In addition to the theatre, the square still has a furniture store, the Spot, a couple of pharmacies, a bank, a small print and office supply shop, a few offices, and the bakery. Gone, however, are the clothing and shoe shops, the jewelry store, and the carpet and flooring store. Similarly, the Index, otherwise known as "the dime store," a staple of the town's business district since 1933, had been gradually reducing its floor space until it finally closed in 1997. A few of the businesses from the square have been replaced by similar businesses on the edges of town. The irony is that Sullivan does not have a Wal-mart or K-Mart, or even any strip malls. Most residents just do not question or hesitate driving twenty to thirty miles to fulfill their needs.

Just because storefronts do not house retail establishments, however, does not mean they are empty. The Little Theatre is using some of these empty buildings for its scene and costume shops and work space. A few of the former Friends, people who had supported the theatre financially for most of the 1980s and early 1990s, have purchased the vacant properties and donated their use to the theatre.

In addition to theatre-friendly parties having control over a portion of the business district, the theatre actually has all of its ancillary functions within yards of, rather than miles from, the theatre.

The theatre's excess space is also fitting into its future outreach and education plans. During the fall of 1997, the theatre, in cooperation with Sullivan Civic Center (an athletic facility run by the city's parks and recreation department), offered dance and movement classes to children and adults. The classes are taught by people affiliated with the theatre and have generated active interest and participation.

While the idea of turning the courthouse square into a theatre camp may be a novel one and is actually considered possible by some of the more ardent theatre supporters, it does not rest well with the "city fathers." The city council's agreement to give the theatre financial help once does not mean the members are either theatre supporters or that they understand the special needs of a nonprofit cultural institution. In addition, the mayor at the time seemed to find the theatre in his town more of an annoyance than an advantage.

Interviewed in 1997, Leon Lane, mayor of Sullivan for twenty of the last thirty years, said he considered the theatre to be good because it brought people into town, but he questioned its economic impact. The same is true for employment. Lane said that, while the theatre may create some local employment, it would not be at the same level as a new industry. In addition, the theatre may attract some people to town but has never attracted industries. "I've never had any industry say they would come to Sullivan because of the theatre," said Lane.

Although Sullivan does have a handful of moderate to large employers—including the Illinois Masonic Home and Agri-Fab, one of two producers in the United States of rotary mowers—the town's future as something other than a bedroom community seems in question. Sullivan continues to attract new residents, and construction of new homes is brisk, but these homes are primarily outside the city limits. It is possible for one to live beyond the southern edge of Sullivan, commute to Mattoon to work, and have little or no contact with the community.

Griffin Smith Jr. (1989) pondered the survivability of small towns in a postindustrial, virtual community society. "We remember small towns as places of contentment and stability . . . ; places where

people had a sense of common purpose and shared values . . ."
(188). Sullivan still has much of this, but the shared values among
many have changed. Instead of taking pride in Sullivan as a unique
community, many acknowledge the fact that the town does not have
the same problems as a larger city.

Smith continued that for many American small towns caught in
the late-twentieth-century whirlwind of social and economic change,
survival has come easiest to those "that have devised new purposes
for themselves" (189–91). This is something Sullivan has yet to do.
Many consider the surrounding area to be a blossoming tourist area,
with Lake Shelbyville ten miles to the south, Amish country fifteen
miles to the east, and Sullivan, with The Little Theatre, in the middle.
This is complemented by the idea that driving two hundred miles
from Chicago to spend a weekend in the country is not unreasonable.

For others, however, the very notion of Moultrie County as a
tourist destination is laughable. An often-repeated phrase was "Sullivan . . . a great place to live but I wouldn't want to visit." And
if one did decide to visit Sullivan without benefit of hosting
friends or family, the area still suffers from the age-old lack of accommodations. Conditions are better than when Guy Little opened
the theatre in 1957, but not enough to support a robust tourist
industry.

Lake Shelbyville does attract thousands of visitors every year, but,
again, it is possible to fish, boat, et cetera, and do little more than
drive through Sullivan. In addition, people who are attracted to the
lake are not necessarily theatergoers. In the meantime, The Little
Theatre On The Square and Sullivan, Illinois, will continue to play
a tug of war between the theatre as a source of community pride
and a grudging acknowledgement that the theatre *may* benefit the
area, that is if nothing else can be found.

The Little Theatre On The Square is most unusual for a town
like Sullivan and, consequently, has changed the community. Sullivan was not a place accustomed to summer stock, and the theatre shocked residents because it was so different. This difference
was compounded by the theatre having been started in an era before cable television, the Internet, and multicultural awareness. Very
early on, Guy Little, as theatre owner and producer, made his hometown—a homogeneous, isolated farming community—deal with
welcoming, housing, and watching onstage other people who very

obviously were not like its inhabitants. Sullivanites could have re-acted much differently but, from all accounts, generally lived up to the community's reputation as hospitable to outsiders and more enlightened than other small towns. This atmosphere allowed a tradition that grew as the theatre succeeded and is evident in the transmogrification of the term "showdog."

The other side of the perspective is that Sullivan merely changed with the surrounding world and that the theatre had nothing do to with the inevitable. True, the theatre did not affect whether or when Sullivan got cable television or other instant-access media. Indeed, many other small towns became wired at the same time. What the theatre did do for Sullivan is to make the community face the inescapable much sooner and with a broader point of view.

Sullivan currently faces many new challenges: remaining eco-nomically vital, meeting changing needs of its residents, and re-minding the world it is still alive. These are the same problems faced by scores, if not hundreds, of other small Midwestern towns. It is doubtful Sullivan will ever just roll up its welcome mat, but any-thing just shy of that is still in question. In the meantime, Sullivan's theatre—and the people associated with it—still bring to a (now) two-stoplight community something decidedly and wonderfully out of the ordinary.

APPENDIXES
BIBLIOGRAPHY
INDEX

Appendix A

PRODUCTIONS AND STARS AT
THE LITTLE THEATRE ON THE SQUARE, 1957–1997

The Little Theatre On The Square featured stars through the 1984 season, operating under a standard contract with Actors Equity Association. In 1985, the theatre switched to a small professional theatre contract, taking advantage of a new contract category created by Equity the preceding year to help small theatres remain economically viable and part of Equity.

Year	Production	Star
1957	*Brigadoon*	Ronald Rogers
1957	*Wonderful Town*	Barbara Terry
1957	*Roberta*	Maureen Reidy
1957	*Kiss Me, Kate*	Jerili Little
1957	*Song of Norway*	Gordon Howard
1957	*Call Me Madam*	Andrea Blayne
1957	*Wish You Were Here*	Paul Barry
1957	*Finian's Rainbow*	Art Ostrin
1957	*Guys and Dolls*	Ronald Rogers
1958	*Pajama Game*	Frank Bouley
1958	*Annie Get Your Gun*	Jerili Little
1958	*Show Boat*	Ronald Rogers
1958	*King and I*	Andrea Blayne
1958	*Boy Friend*	Jerili Little
1958	*Plain and Fancy*	Andrea Blayne

1958	*Can-Can*	Andrea Blayne
1958	*Desert Song*	Paul Flores
1958	*Damn Yankees*	Robert Gwaltney
1958	*Oklahoma!*	Paul Flores
1959	*Bells Are Ringing*	Mike Rayhill
1959	*Kismet*	Ronald Rogers
1959	*Guys and Dolls*	Alan Alda
1959	*Student Prince*	Greta Wolff
1959	*Say Darling*	Ted Lawrie
1959	*High Button Shoes*	Art Ostrin
1959	*Naughty Marietta*	Joan Sena
1959	*Song of Norway*	Annamary Dickey
1959	*Gentlemen Prefer Blondes*	Jerili Little
1959	*Fanny*	Betty Oakes
1960	*South Pacific*	Bruce Foote
1960	*Pal Joey*	Ruth Warrick
1960	*Tree Grows in Brooklyn*	Margaret Hamilton
1960	*Li'l Abner*	Alan Alda
1960	*Carousel*	L. D. Clements
1960	*West Side Story*	Gretta Wolff
1960	*Redhead*	Jerili Little
1961	*Take Me Along*	Annamary Dickey
1961	*Brigadoon*	Jack Haskell
1961	*Paint Your Wagon*	Rosemary Prinz
1961	*Bloomer Girl*	Margaret Hamilton
1961	*Merry Widow*	Dolores Wilson
1961	*Anything Goes*	Robert Gwaltney
1961	*Flower Drum Song*	Sylvia Copeland
1962	*Tunnel of Love*	Eddie Bracken
1962	*Glass Menagerie*	Mark Rydell
1962	*King and I*	Dolores Wilson
1962	*Bye Bye Birdie*	Jack Chaplain
1962	*Oklahoma!*	Peter Palmer
1962	*Gypsy*	Margaret Whiting
1962	*Music Man*	Jeff Warren
1963	*Harvey*	Joe E. Brown
1963	*Blithe Spirit*	Marjorie Lord
1963	*Critics Choice*	Bernard Grant
1963	*Late Love*	Margaret Truman

1963	*Carnival*	Jerili Little
1963	*Unsinkable Molly Brown*	Rosemary Prinz
1963	*Everybody Loves Opal*	Ann B. Davis
1963	*Miss Pell Is Missing*	Edward Everett Horton
1963	*Dear Ruth*	Pat O'Brien and Eloise O'Brien
1963	*Tender Trap*	Peter Palmer
1964	*Kind Sir*	Rosemary Prinz
1964	*Seven Year Itch*	Eddie Bracken
1964	*Solid Gold Cadillac*	Marvin Miller and Violet Carlson
1964	*Sound of Music*	Betty Ann Grove
1964	*My Fair Lady*	Jerili Little and Richard Gray
1964	*Pajama Game*	Peter Palmer
1964	*Happiest Years*	David Nelson
1964	*Lo and Behold!*	Marie Wilson
1964	*Janus*	Linda Darnell
1964	*Come Blow Your Horn*	Jack Ging
1964	*Stop the World— I Want to Get Off*	Larry Holofcener
1965	*Ready When You Are, C.B.!*	Kathleen Nolan
1965	*King of Hearts*	Don Hastings
1965	*Sunday in New York*	Gary Conway and Christina Crawford
1965	*Gigi*	Margaret O'Brien
1965	*Dracula*	John Carradine
1965	*Bus Stop*	Edd Byrnes
1965	*Mister Roberts*	Tab Hunter
1965	*Here's Love*	Julia Meade
1965	*Camelot*	Betty Ann Grove
1965	*110 in the Shade*	Peter Palmer
1965	*Love and Kisses*	Pat O'Brien and Eloise O'Brien
1965	*Mary, Mary*	Rosemary Prinz
1965	*Funny Thing Happened on the Way to the Forum*	John Kelso
1965	*Irma La Douce*	Jerili Little and Art Ostrin
1965	*Goodbye, Ghost*	June Allyson

1966	*Lullaby*	Rosemary Prinz
1966	*Timid Tiger*	John Payne
1966	*Catch Me If You Can*	Dennis Weaver
1966	*World of Suzie Wong*	Robert Reed
1966	*Oliver*	John Carradine
1966	*Carousel*	Peter Palmer
1966	*Allegro*	Annamary Dickey
1966	*She Loves Me*	Julius La Rosa
1966	*How to Succeed in Business Without Really Trying*	Stuart Erwin
1966	*Never Too Late*	Andy Devine
1966	*Any Wednesday*	Elinor Donahue
1966	*Moon Is Blue*	Carl Betz
1966	*Strictly Dishonorable*	Cesar Romero
1967	*Barefoot in the Park*	Tab Hunter
1967	*Odd Couple*	Alan Young
1967	*You Can't Take It with You*	Santos Ortega
1967	*Life with Father*	Mary Stuart
1967	*On a Clear Day You Can See Forever*	Jack Haskell
1967	*Show Boat*	Bruce Yarnell
1967	*Funny Girl*	Gardner McKay
1967	*Sweet Charity*	Will Hutchins
1967	*South Pacific*	Betty Ann Grove
1967	*Voice of the Turtle*	Terry Moore
1967	*My Three Angels*	Andy Devine
1967	*Who's Afraid of Virginia Woolf?*	Mercedes McCambridge
1967	*Girl Could Get Lucky*	Rosemary Prinz
1968	*Marriage-Go-Round*	Vivian Vance
1968	*Picnic*	Robert Horton
1968	*Generation*	Robert Cummings
1968	*Glad Tidings*	Ann Sothern
1968	*What Did We Do Wrong?*	Pat O'Brien and Eloise O'Brien
1968	*Student Prince*	Peter Palmer
1968	*Guys and Dolls*	Jean Kean
1968	*Sound of Music*	Dorothy Collins
1968	*Oklahoma!*	Bruce Yarnell

1968	Kiss Me, Kate	Patricia Morison
1968	No Time for Sergeants	Peter Marshall
1968	Miracle Worker	Katharine Houghton
1968	Under the Yum-Yum Tree	Jack Haskell
1968	Owl and the Pussycat	Eileen Fulton and Tom Poston
1969	Cactus Flower	Joan Caufield and Anthony George
1969	Impossible Years	Durward Kirby
1969	Private Ear and the Public Eye	Katharine Houghton
1969	Holiday for Lovers	Pat O'Brien and Eloise O'Brien
1969	Teahouse of the August Moon	Ron Ely
1969	Annie Get Your Gun	Rosemary Prinz
1969	Do I Hear A Waltz?	Patricia Morison
1969	George M!	Bill Hayes
1969	Pal Joey	Margaret Whiting
1969	Music Man	Peter Palmer and Aniko Palmer
1969	You Know I Can't Hear You When the Water's Running	Imogene Coca and King Donovan
1969	Cat on a Hot Tin Roof	Eileen Fulton
1969	Dial "M" for Murder	Jonathan Frid
1970	Thousand Clowns	James Drury
1970	Born Yesterday	Betty Grable
1970	Critic's Choice	Ray Milland
1970	Something Different	Alan Sues
1970	Little Me	Harvey Korman
1970	Cabaret	Meredith MacRae
1970	Man of La Mancha	Bruce Yarnell
1970	Mame	Gisele MacKenzie
1970	Brigadoon	Peter Palmer and Aniko Palmer
1970	Don't Drink the Water	Imogene Coca and King Donovan
1970	Streetcar Named Desire	David Canary
1970	Star-Spangled Girl	Eileen Fulton

1970	*Boeing-Boeing*	Lyle Waggoner
1971	*Paisley Convertible*	Bill Bixby
1971	*Beginner's Luck*	Bob Crane
1971	*There's a Girl in My Soup*	Van Johnson
1971	*Mousetrap*	Noel Harrison
1971	*Plaza Suite*	Durward Kirby
1971	*Great Waltz*	Marion Marlowe
1971	*Hello, Dolly!*	Virginia Mayo
1971	*Most Happy Fella*	Bruce Yarnell
1971	*Fiddler on the Roof*	Tom Poston
1971	*Li'l Abner*	Peter Palmer
1971	*Play It Again, Sam*	Pat Paulsen
1971	*Here Today*	Gisele MacKenzie
1971	*Private Lives*	Jeanne Crain
1971	*You're A Good Man, Charlie Brown*	
1971	*Champagne Complex*	Don Ameche
1972	*I Do! I Do!*	Rosemary Prinz and David Canary
1972	*Forty Carats*	June Lockhart
1972	*Paris Is Out*	Pat O'Brien and Eloise O'Brien
1972	*13 Rue de L'Amour*	Rosemary Prinz and Tom Poston
1972	*Under Papa's Picture*	Eve Arden
1972	*1776*	Bill Hayes
1972	*Unsinkable Molly Brown*	Barbara Rush
1972	*Anything Goes*	Frank Sutton
1972	*Fiddler on the Roof*	Shelley Berman
1972	*Promises, Promises*	Peter Palmer
1972	*Company*	Janis Paige and Ed Evanko
1972	*Lion in Winter*	Helen Wagner and Donald May
1972	*Last of the Red Hot Lovers*	Rosemary Prinz
1972	*Help Stamp Out Marriage*	Van Johnson
1973	*Goodbye, Charlie*	JoAnne Worley
1973	*Butterflies Are Free*	Virginia Graham
1973	*Here Lies Jeremy Troy*	George Maharis

1973	*Charley's Aunt*	Dick Sargent
1973	*Irma La Douce*	Lesley Ann Warren
1973	*Damn Yankees*	Gary Collins
1973	*Camelot*	George Chakiris
1973	*Applause*	Rosemary Prinz
1973	*Fantasticks*	Bill Hayes
1973	*On a Clear Day You Can See Forever*	Harve Presnell
1973	*Blossom Time*	Allan Jones
1973	*Blithe Spirit*	Ann Miller and Margaret Hamilton
1973	*Wait until Dark*	Michael Cole
1974	*Hair*	
1974	*One Flew over the Cuckoo's Nest*	Leonard Nimoy
1974	*Lovers and Other Strangers*	Dennis Cole and Helen Wagner
1974	*Sugar*	Robert Morse
1974	*Mame*	Rosemary Prinz
1974	*Funny Girl*	Mimi Hines
1974	*No, No, Nanette*	Andy Devine
1974	*Gigi*	Jean Pierre Aumont
1974	*Oklahoma!*	Peter Palmer and Aniko Palmer
1974	*Prisoner of Second Avenue*	Shelley Berman
1974	*Twigs*	Rosemary Prinz
1975	*Godspell*	
1975	*Gypsy*	Rosemary Prinz
1975	*Jesus Christ Superstar*	
1975	*My Fair Lady*	George Chakiris
1975	*Sound of Music*	Peter Palmer and Aniko Palmer
1975	*Torch Bearers*	Fannie Flagg
1975	*Sleuth*	Keir Dullea
1976	*Two of Us*	Bill Hayes and Susan Seaforth Hayes
1976	*Three Goats and a Blanket*	Mickey Rooney
1976	*Music Man*	Michael Callan

1976	*1776*	Robert Conrad
1976	*Show Boat*	Forrest Tucker
1976	*Hello, Dolly!*	Sue Ane Langdon
1976	*George Washington Slept Here*	Peggy Cass
1977	*Eileen Fulton Show*	Eileen Fulton
1977	*And Mama Makes Three*	Isabel Sanford
1977	*Most Marvelous News*	Eve Arden
1977	*Fiddler on the Roof*	Stubby Kaye
1977	*Once upon a Mattress*	Sue Ane Langdon
1977	*Shenandoah*	John Saxon
1977	*Shenandoah*	David Canary
1977	*Equus*	John Gavin
1977	*Mary, Mary*	Rosemary Prinz
1977	*Vanities*	Maeve McGuire, Marie Masters, and Judith Chapman
1977	*Eileen Fulton Show* (TV taping)	Eileen Fulton
1978	*I Do! I Do!*	Peter Palmer and Aniko Palmer
1978	*Oh, Coward!*	Kathryn Crosby
1978	*Man of La Mancha*	John Saxon
1978	*Marriage-Go-Round*	Kitty Carlisle
1978	*Dracula*	John Phillip Law
1978	*Cabaret*	Russ Tamblyn
1978	*Star-Spangled Girl*	Dennis Cooney and Marie Masters
1979	*California Suite*	Marie Masters
1979	*Pippin*	Eddie Mekka
1979	*Little Night Music*	Arlene Dahl
1979	*Little Mary Sunshine*	Patrice Munsel
1979	*Wait Until Dark*	Betsy Palmer
1981	*Same Time, Next Year*	Kathryn Hays
1981	*Big Bad Burlesque*	
1981	*Butterflies Are Free*	Rue McClanahan
1981	*Never Too Late*	Hans Conreid
1981	*Grease*	

1982	*Chapter Two*	Rosemary Prinz
1982	*Oklahoma!*	John Wesley Shipp
1982	*I Love My Wife*	Nicolette Goulet
1982	*Deathtrap*	Bernard Barrow and Larry Breeding
1982	*Mass Appeal*	Gavin McLeod
1983	*Dames at Sea*	Eddie Mekka and Denise Lively Mekka
1983	*They're Playing Our Song*	Colleen Zenk
1983	*Fantasticks*	Robert Newman
1983	*Something's Afoot*	Kathryn Grayson
1983	*Annie*	
1983	*Sharon Carlson Show*	Sharon Carlson
1984	*Tintypes*	Sheila MacRae
1984	*Two by Two*	Larry Storch
1984	*Pump Boys and Dinettes*	Stephen McNaughton
1984	*Oliver*	Louis Edmonds
1984	*Carnival*	Terri Eoff
1985	*Funny Thing Happened on the Way to the Forum*	
1985	*Bleacher Bums*	
1985	*1940s Radio Hour*	
1985	*Good Doctor*	
1985	*South Pacific*	
1985	*Cotton Patch Gospel*	
1986	*Guys and Dolls*	
1986	*Rainmaker*	
1986	*Day in Hollywood, Night in the Ukraine*	
1986	*Harvey*	
1986	*Man of La Mancha*	
1987	*Little Shop of Horrors*	
1987	*Chorus Line*	
1987	*Fiddler on the Roof*	
1987	*Sound of Music*	
1987	*Best Little Whorehouse in Texas*	
1988	*Sugar Babies*	

1988	*Joseph and the Amazing Technicolor Dreamcoat*	
1988	*Seven Brides for Seven Brothers*	
1988	*42nd Street*	
1988	*My One and Only*	
1989	*Little Me*	
1989	*Drood*	
1989	*Hello, Dolly!*	
1989	*Baby*	
1989	*King and I*	
1990	*Music Man*	Bill Hayes
1990	*Anything Goes*	
1990	*My Fair Lady*	
1990	*Gypsy*	
1990	*Nunsense*	
1991	*I Do! I Do!*	
1991	*Oklahoma!*	
1991	*Camelot*	
1991	*Annie Get Your Gun*	
1991	*Me and My Girl*	
1991	*South Pacific*	
1992	*Living, Loving, Laughing*	
1992	*Singin' in the Rain*	
1992	*Big River*	
1992	*Sweet Charity*	
1992	*West Side Story*	
1992	*Best Little Whorehouse in Texas*	
1992	*Ben and Teddy Show*	
1993	*Meet Me in St. Louis*	
1993	*Cabaret*	
1993	*Noises Off*	
1993	*Do Black Patent Leather Shoes Really Reflect Up?*	
1993	*Phantom*	
1994	*Carousel*	
1994	*Sugar*	

1994   *Odd Couple*
1994   *Babes in Arms*
1994   *Nunsense II*
1995   *Ziegfeld, a Night at the Follies*
1995   *1940s Radio Hour*
1995   *Lend Me a Tenor*
1995   *Fiddler on the Roof*
1995   *Damn Yankees*
1996   *Will Rogers Follies*
1996   *Guys and Dolls*
1996   *Foreigner*
1996   *Funny Thing Happened on
          the Way to the Forum*
1996   *Monkey Business*
1997   *Sugar Babies*
1997   *Brigadoon*
1997   *Forever Plaid*
1997   *Crazy for You*
1997   *Godspell*

THE MOST FREQUENTLY PRODUCED SHOWS AT THE LITTLE THEATRE ON THE SQUARE AND THE NUMBER OF TIMES PRODUCED, 1957–1997

Production	Frequency
Oklahoma!	6
Fiddler on the Roof	5
Guys and Dolls	5
Brigadoon	4
Music Man	4
Sound of Music	4
South Pacific	4
Annie Get Your Gun	3
Anything Goes	3
Cabaret	3
Camelot	3
Carousel	3
Damn Yankees	3
Funny Thing Happened on the Way to the Forum	3
Gypsy	3
Hello, Dolly!	3
I Do! I Do!	3
King and I	3
Man of La Mancha	3
My Fair Lady	3
Show Boat	3

BIBLIOGRAPHY

Actors Equity Association. 1993. Rules Governing Employment in Small Professional Theatres. New York.

Althoff, Shirley. 1966. "The Miracle of Sullivan." *St Louis Globe Democrat Sunday Magazine,* 13 September, 6–12.

Ames, David L. 1995. "Interpreting Post–World War II Suburban Landscapes as Historic Resources." *Preserving the Recent Past.* Edited by Deborah Slaton and Rebecca Shiffer, 97–102. Washington, D.C.: Historic Preservation Education Foundation.

Berkowitz, Gerald M. 1982. *New Broadways: Theatre Across America, 1950–1980.* Totawa, N.J.: Rowman and Littlefield.

Calthorpe, Peter. 1993. *The Next American Metropolis: Ecology, Community, and the American Dream.* Princeton: Princeton Architectural Press.

Cavanaugh, Tom. 1968. "How to Succeed in Show Business by Really Trying." *Marathon World,* Fall.

Conroy, Frank. 1993. Foreword to *Small Town America: The Missouri Photo Workshops, 1949–1991,* by Cliff Edom, Vi Edom, Verna May Edom Smith. Golden, Colo.: Fulcrum.

Ehrenhalt, Alan. 1996. "Return to Main Street." *Governing* 9 (May):18–27.

Eisenberg, Alan. 1984. "Equity's State of the Union: Actors Union Reports Its Status and Sets Its Goals." *Variety,* 11 January.

Francaviglia, Richard V. 1996. *Main Street Revisited: Time, Space, and Image Building in Small-Town America.* Iowa City: University of Iowa Press.

Fulton, Eileen. 1970. *How My World Turns.* New York: Taplinger.

———. 1995. *As My World Still Turns.* Secaucus, N.J.: Birch Lane.

Gard, Robert E., Marston Balch, and Pauline B. Temkin. 1968. *Theater in America: Appraisal and Challenge for the National Theatre Conference.* Madison: Dembar Educational Research Services; New York: Theatre Arts Books.

Gard, Robert E., and Gertrude S. Burley. 1959. *Community Theatre: Idea and Achievement.* New York: Duell, Sloan and Pearce.

Gould, Peter, and Rodney White. 1986. *Mental Maps.* 2nd ed. Boston: Allen and Unwin.

Hecht, Stuart J. 1992. "The Plays of Alice Gerstenberg: Cultural Hegemony in the American Little Theatre." *Journal of Popular Culture* 26, no. 1:1–16.

Hokanson, Drake. 1994. *Reflecting a Prairie Town: A Year in Peterson.* Iowa City: University of Iowa Press.

Horn, Barbara Lee. 1982. *"Hair:* Changing Versions." Ph.D. diss., City University of New York.

Hummler, Richard. 1988. "Equity's Small Pro Theatre Pact Boosting Work for Local Actors." *Variety,* 23 November, 99.

Illinois Arts Council. 1996. Program Grant Application 1996–1997. Applicant: The Little Theatre On The Square, Inc. Chicago.

———. 1997. Established Regional Arts Institutions Application—FY98. Applicant: The Little Theatre On The Square, Inc. Chicago.

Illinois Department of Commerce and Community Affairs. 1986. Illinois Small Business Development Program. Designee: City of Sullivan. Springfield.

———. 1991. Tourism Attraction Grant Program Application. Applicant: The Little Theatre On The Square, Inc. Springfield.

Illinois Department of Revenue. 1979. "Reporting Receipts from Retailer's Occupation Tax, Service Occupation Tax, Use Tax: Amounts Collected for Municipalities and Counties Excluded." *Quarterly Report.* Springfield.

———. 1980. "Reporting Receipts from Retailer's Occupation Tax, Service Occupation Tax, Use Tax: Amounts Collected for Municipalities and Counties Excluded." *Quarterly Report.* Springfield.

———. 1981. "Reporting Receipts from Retailer's Occupation Tax, Service Occupation Tax, Use Tax: Amounts Collected for Municipalities and Counties Excluded." *Quarterly Report.* Springfield.

Jackson, John Brinckerhoff. 1994. *A Sense of Place, A Sense of Time.* New Haven: Yale University Press.

Joy, John F. 1975. "American Theatre of the Sixties: An Inside View." Ph.D. diss., Carnegie-Mellon University.

Key, Nancy Martin. 1987. "A Narrative History of Lake Charles Little Theatre, Lake Charles, Louisiana, 1927–1982." Ph.D. diss., New York University.

Kroll, Jack. 1967. "Making of a Theatre," *Newsweek,* 13 November, 124–25.

———. 1968. "Hairpiece," *Newsweek,* 13 May, 110.

Langley, Stephen. 1990. *Theatre Management and Production in America: Commercial, Stock, Resident, College, Community, and Presenting Organizations.* New York: Drama Book Publishers.

Lingeman, Richard. 1980. *Small Town America: A Narrative History, 1620–Present.* Boston: Houghton Mifflin.

Macgowan, Kenneth. 1969. *Footlights Across America: Towards a National Theater.* New York: Harcourt, Brace, 1929. Reprint, New York: Kraus Reprint.

Martin, R. Eden. 1996. *The Whitley Point Record Book: The Justice of the Peace Docket Book, Estray List and Country Store Record of the Earliest Settlement in Moultrie County, Illinois.* Chicago: R. Eden Martin.

Neal, Arthur G. 1998. *National Trauma and Collective Memory: Major Events in the American Century.* Armonk, N.Y.: M. E. Sharpe.

Oldenburg, Ray. 1997. *The Great Good Place: Cafes, Coffee Shops, Community Centers, Beauty Parlors, General Stores, Bars, Hangouts and How They Get You Through the Day.* 2nd ed. New York: Marlowe.

Papp, Joseph. 1988. "The Age of Aquarius." *New York,* 11 April, 54–55.

Pindell, Terry. 1995. *A Good Place to Live: America's Last Migration.* New York: Henry Holt.

Price, Edward T. 1986. "The Central Courthouse Square in the American County Seat." *Geographical Review,* January 1968. Reprint, *Common Places: Reading in American Vernacular Architecture.* Edited by Dell Upton and John Michael Vlach. Athens: University of London Press.

Quinney, Richard. 1986. "A Traveler on Country Roads." *Landscape* 29, no. 1:21–28.

Ryden, Kent C. 1993. *Mapping the Invisible Landscape: Folklore, Writing, and the Sense of Place.* Iowa City: University of Iowa Press.

Smith, Griffin, Jr. 1989. "Small-Town America: An Endangered Species?" *National Geographic* 175 (February):186–215.

Spriggs, Robert William. 1983. Samuel Rufus Harshman: Nineteenth Century South-Central Illinois Holiness Man. Ph.D. diss., St. Louis University.

Sullivan: Remember When? 1992. Vol. 3. Sullivan, Ill.: Moultrie County Genealogical and Historical Society.

Thomajan, P. K. 1939. "Temportraits: Annamary Dickey." *Musician* 5 (May):87.

Twenty-Five Seasons of Shows and Stars: The Little Theatre on the Square. 1982. Sullivan, Ill: Friends of The Little Theatre, Inc.

U.S. Bureau of the Census. [1903?]. *U.S. Census of Population: 1900.* Vol. 1, *Characteristics of the Population.* Part 15, *Illinois.* Washington, D.C.: U.S. Government Printing Office.

———. 1952. *U.S. Census of Population: 1950*. Vol. 2, *Characteristics of the Population*. Part 13, *Illinois*. Washington, D.C.: U.S. Government Printing Office.

———. 1963. *U.S. Census of Population: 1960*. Vol. 1, *Characteristics of the Population*. Part 15, *Illinois*. Washington, D.C.: U.S. Government Printing Office.

———. 1992. *U.S. Census of Population: 1990*. *General Population Characteristics, Illinois*. Washington, D.C.: U.S. Government Printing Office.

U.S. Department of the Interior. 1995. *National Park Service National Register of Historic Places. Moultrie County Courthouse*. Washington, D.C.: U.S. Government Printing Office.

Warrick, Ruth. 1980. *The Confessions of Phoebe Tyler*. Englewood Cliffs, N.J.: Prentice-Hall.

Zelinsky, Wilbur. 1988. "Where Every Town Is Above Average: Welcoming Signs along America's Highways." *Landscape* 30, no. 1:1–10.

INTERVIEWS AND CORRESPONDENCE

Except as noted, interviews were conducted in Sullivan, Illinois.

Anderson, Leonard A. Interview, 3 August 1996.

Bell, Charles. Interview, 4 August 1996.

Best, Emilee R. Interview, 5 August 1996.

Best, Marion. Interview, 12 August 1997.

Fehr, David. Letter, 21 May 1997.

Florini, Jean. Interview, 19 June 1996.

Florini, Jibby. Interview, 20 June 1996.

Florini, Joe. Interview, 19 June 1996.

Florini, Ruth. Interview, 20 June 1996.

Haws, Michael. Interview, 3 August 1996.

Hollowell, Margaret C. Interview, Charleston, Ill., 21 June 1996.

Isaacs, Richard J. Interview, 20 June 1996.

Lane, Leon. Interview, 15 August 1997.

Milo, Jack. Interview, 20 June 1996.

Mobley, David. Interview, Mattoon, Ill., 21 June 1996.

Palmer, Mamie. Interview, 5 August 1996.

Reines, M. Seth. Interview, 3 August 1996.

Rowles, Pauline. Interview, 20 June 1996.

Simon, Paul. Letter, 29 July 1997.

Stubblefield, Marilyn. Interview, 19 June 1996.

Stubblefield, William. Interview, 19 June 1996.

White, Ronald. Interview, 5 August 1996.
White, Sharon. Interview, 18 June 1996.
York, Lee. Electronic mail, 25 and 27 August 1997.

INDEX

Beth Conway Shervey completed her doctorate in American Culture Studies from Bowling Green State University in 1998. She spent her early years in Sullivan and worked at The Little Theatre On The Square.